Funding the architectural heritage: a guide to policies and examples

Robert Pickard

Council of Europe Publishing

French edition:
Financement du patrimoine architectural: analyse des politiques et des pratiques
(forthcoming)

Cover design: Document and Publications Production Department, Council of Europe
Illustrations: Robert Pickard

Council of Europe Publishing
F-67075 Strasbourg Cedex
http://book.coe.int

ISBN 978-92-871-6498-8
© Council of Europe, 2009
Printed at the Council of Europe

Contents

Acknowledgements

The author would like to acknowledge the following people and organisations that assisted the production of this text:

Jadran Antolović, State Secretary, Ministry of Culture, Croatia

Athena Aristotelous-Cleridou, Head of Conservation Section, Department of Town Planning and Housing, Cyprus

Michael Auer, National Park Service, US Department of Interior, Washington DC, USA

Peter Baars, National Restoration Fund, Amsterdam, Netherlands

Clotilde Desalbres, Université Paris 1, France

Duncan Frazer, City of Edmonton, Historic Resource Management Programme, Canada

Pierre Laurent Frier, Université Paris 1, France

Jérôme Fromageau, Faculté Jean Monnet, Université Paris Sud, France

Edgar Goedleven, Director of Monuments, Flanders Region, Brussels, Belgium

Christopher Grayson, Parliamentary Assembly of the Council of Europe

A.G. Van Houten, Hendrick de Keyser Foundation (private foundation), Amsterdam, Netherlands

Erik Huber, BYFO, Copenhagen, Denmark

C. Huijts, Stadsherstel Amsterdam NV, Amsterdam, Netherlands

Christian Ibsen, Ministry of Housing and Urban Renewal, Denmark

Wolfgang Illert, Brandenburgische Schlösser GmbH, Potsdam, Germany

Brian Jobson, Tyne and Wear Building Preservation Trust Ltd, Newcastle upon Tyne, UK

Carsten Lund, National Forest and Nature Agency, Copenhagen, Denmark

Ulla Lunn, National Forest and Nature Agency, Copenhagen, Denmark

Bill MacCrostie, E and Y Kenneth Leventhal Real Estate, Washington DC, USA

Alexander Melissinos, Architect-Urbanist, Paris, France

Tracy Pickerill, Dublin Institute of Technology, Ireland

Jelka Pirkovic, State Secretary, Ministry of Culture, Government of Slovenia

Mark Pitzer, Internal Revenue Service, Washington DC, USA

Erik Rosenkrans, BYFO, Copenhagen, Denmark

Royal Institution of Chartered Surveyors Education Trust, UK

Dan Sanders, Department of Environmental Protection, New Jersey, USA

Ursula Schirmer, Deutsche Stiftung Denkmalkschutz, Bonn, Germany

John Schmalz, Coopers and Lybrand, Washington DC, USA

Celia Tazelaar, Department of Environmental Protection, New Jersey, USA

Robert Totaro, Pennrose Properties, Philadelphia, USA

John Weiler, Heritage Canada Foundation, Ottawa, Canada

1. Architectural heritage funding issues

1.0. Introduction

The aim of this publication is to identify opportunities for the mobilisation of financial resources for conservation, restoration, rehabilitation and management of the architectural heritage, drawing on examples from Europe and North America.

There is a need to increase private investment, which is only likely to be achieved according to the principles of profitability, which govern the free operation of the market.

The sustainable approach should be for tax mechanisms and credit policies to favour conservation and use – rehabilitation – in housing policy or in the establishment of business and tertiary activities, rather than new construction. This, in turn, supports the idea of a "living" heritage rather than a "museum" heritage. Most historic buildings should be capable of allowing an economic or otherwise beneficial use.

However, it is well recognised that there are limits to the use of private investment in the rehabilitation process, particularly as credit institutions (such as banks) may be reluctant to lend money on old buildings to assist in conservation or rehabilitation work because there are inherent risks as compared to modern property.

The possibility of obtaining a subsidy in addition to private sources of funds or some other form of security can reduce the risk factor and may lead to a more enthusiastic attitude by private sector investors (including individual owners of protected property). Moreover, where housing loan policy in European countries has favoured new construction, there is a need to create a framework more conducive to the operation of the rehabilitation market, which can have other associated socio-economic and cultural benefits when applied to property with recognised heritage value. The aim should be to place both markets on an equal footing.

Legal restrictions on the ownership of property and on investment can also have a negative impact on potential investors in the architectural heritage. In the free market all potential investors should be encouraged.

In some countries the institutions and legal procedures necessary for opening up markets to competition are still developing. Moreover, in the countries-in-transition in central and eastern Europe the question of land and property restitution is still in process – and there may even be a reluctance to return heritage assets to private ownership for fear that the private sector will not accept the responsibility for safeguarding heritage assets.

There may also be a reluctance to allow foreign investors into the market for cultural, philosophical or political reasons. However, the development of appropriate regulations and policies for heritage protection should ensure that all potential owners and users, whether nationals or not, are equally bound in law and equally able to benefit from financial incentives.

1.1. The heritage-funding problem

There are recognised limits on state budgets to support the built heritage. Based on the premise that financial resources are finite and that most governments are unable to provide as much funding as may be needed or desirable, bearing in mind other demands of society, it may be necessary to find arguments to persuade governments to allocate a larger slice of the state budget for this purpose. In this context it is relevant to consider the direct and indirect benefits to be gained from financially supporting the heritage.

Studies have been carried out by ICOMOS and some countries (notably the United Kingdom, Germany and the United States), and reported by the European Union, that reveal the direct and indirect benefits to be gained from investing in the cultural heritage. Direct benefits include the conservation, restoration and rehabilitation of heritage property: long-term preservation. The indirect benefits are much wider. These include the provision of accommodation for living and working, and tax revenues gained as a result of occupation; supporting traditional crafts and professional employment, with the tax revenues gained through people employed in conservation work; tourism and the associated employment, income and tax revenue; and the improvement of facilities and enhancement of the environment to the benefit of society as a whole. Moreover, these studies have consistently shown that public investment in the heritage usually levers a considerably higher amount of investment from the private sector (with resultant tax revenues for the public budget), with an overall gain for the built heritage and a gain for society.

These types of studies are now being used as an argument to generate financial support from public budgets – principally because of the overall benefits that can be gained. However, it is important that funding is directed in a way that will benefit wider society: not necessarily to those built assets that are of the greatest importance, but to those that are endangered. For example, the rehabilitation of older buildings can create opportunities for good housing, as well as preserving a heritage asset. Thus, if it can be argued that preserving architectural heritage will benefit society generally (rather than it being an elitist activity to the benefit of a few), this is more likely to encourage government financial support.

It may be useful to develop "indicators" of benefits (not just relating to preservation) that can be gained from financial support to the heritage, which could be statistically analysed and presented when government budgets are being considered. The possibilities for cultural tourism, the development of enterprises, jobs, and living and business accommodation, the benefits of an improved environment and the resulting tax revenues should all be considered.

1.2. Programmes and strategies, and the use of official incentives for the preservation and enhancement of old buildings and areas

There are two main ways in which governments can take action to encourage conservation, restoration and rehabilitation. The first involves policies and measures to stimulate the private sector to invest in architectural heritage (the dynamic approach). The second derives from the fact that, without government support, the private sector may decide that investment is not economically justified, thus creating the need for financial incentives and subsidies (the support approach).

If both forms of action are considered together, this can be very effective in encouraging investment. For instance, some countries have adopted policy mechanisms focused on areas of architectural, cultural and historic interest, using a form of partnership whereby municipal authorities must devise an action plan for heritage-led revitalisation in order to obtain public funds to support action. Evidence suggests that such programmes can generate six times the initial public investment, or more, through private-sector partners or other sources.

Heritage conservation involves a range of cultural and socio-economic values, each of which needs to be taken into consideration. In the case of monuments, heritage authorities will normally have full regard to cultural values in their conservation work. Where funds are available from public sources, the competent authority will be able direct action to this goal. However, when the implementing agent comes from the private sector, where an important objective is to achieve at least a minimum level of profitability, cultural values will be less important; the objective is more likely to be either to minimise costs or to enhance commercial values. A balance between these differing objectives must be achieved.

Within a sustainable framework, there is a need to balance the requirements of all interested parties: public authorities, private-sector interests and the public at large. Thus some guidelines are necessary, which may be categorised as one of two methods: first, to create a favourable setting for the launching of projects concerning the built heritage; and, second, where financial incentives are made available, to ensure that the mechanisms for protection and enhancement can be more specifically directed.

In general, there is a range of heritage values (cultural, aesthetic, educational, economic, functional and social) and these need not be in conflict. There may be a margin within which the capacity for change can be negotiated (some buildings can be adapted more easily than others). The end result should be an agreement between the relevant heritage and planning authorities and those who would benefit from the intervention in the market, whereby the public benefits from the primary objectives of the whole exercise: sustaining architectural heritage, and creating or furthering a living heritage.

1.3. Raising consciousness

A number of impediments to conservation, restoration and rehabilitation projects by the public sector stem either from a lack of suitable administrative structures or from undue complexity, particularly overtly negative and restrictive control.

An appropriate consciousness-raising policy is essential to encourage owners and developers to invest in conservation and rehabilitation. Such a strategy must emphasise to investors the potential economic value of their asset, which makes it possible to use existing resources and to avoid "wasting" assets. For example, the state department responsible for cultural heritage or the municipal authorities responsible for land-use planning could be encouraged to develop "at risk" registers of endangered historic buildings in their area, on the basis of a brief survey of their condition and occupancy.

A register of this type will assist those who are looking for opportunities to invest in built heritage, focusing attention where it is most needed. Moreover, subsidised surveys to encourage regular maintenance and conservative repair, rather than costly restoration, which in itself can be damaging in terms of authenticity, can be linked to public financial support.

1.4. Council of Europe advice on funding and fiscal measures

This publication builds on previous recommendations, resolutions and conventions that have sought to raise awareness of appropriate forms to be utilised in relation to architectural heritage. These are summarised here.

The first consideration of financial issues by the Council of Europe was through Resolution (66) 20 on the reviving of monuments (adopted by the Ministers' Deputies on 29 March 1966), which urged governments to provide fiscal (tax relief) and financial measures (loans and grants) to assist owners of monuments and other bodies to protect architectural heritage.

Following the discussion of financial issues at the Congress on European Architectural Heritage (Amsterdam, 21-25 October 1975), the Congress's Amsterdam Declaration included a more extensive description of financial measures, which was put forward in Resolution (76) 28 concerning the adaptation of laws and regulations to the requirements of integrated conservation of the architectural heritage (adopted by the Committee of Ministers on 14 April 1976).

These included the reallocation of funds via national budgetary policies, from redevelopment and construction schemes to become more evenly in favour of rehabilitation of architectural heritage, using official financial aid mechanisms and practical arrangements to support publicly managed and privately owned architectural heritage. Specific measures included:

- financing of preliminary surveys (to obtain the information needed for drafting programmes for the integrated conservation of monuments and groups of buildings);
- grants (both repayable and non-repayable) to help public and private owners restore or rehabilitate buildings;
- tax relief to enable to owners to devote more of their means to maintenance and conservation (including reductions in property tax, the setting-off of maintenance and restoration costs against income tax, and reductions in estate tax); and,
- the establishment of a "revolving fund".

The need to consider financial measures in laws on architectural heritage was made a requirement of signatory countries to the Convention for the Protection of the Architectural Heritage, the Granada Convention (Granada, 3-4 October 1985; ETS No. 121).

Under Articles 6.1 and 6.2 of the convention, each party is required to provide appropriate financial support measures, including fiscal measures if necessary. The explanatory report to the Granada Convention emphasised that the burden of conserving an even more extensive heritage should be shared by the community as a whole: "it cannot be borne by public authorities alone".

Article 14 further identified the need to foster the development of:

- sponsorship; and
- non-profit-making associations.

Detailed advice on financial support measures was subsequently provided in Recommendation No. R (91) 6 on measures likely to support the funding of the conservation of the architectural heritage (adopted by the Committee of Ministers on 9 September 1991) and through a Council of Europe publication entitled *Funding the Architectural Heritage* published later in 1991. These were summarised in a companion volume to the compendium of texts of the Council of Europe in the field of cultural heritage as follows:

i. Administrative measures

In order to create favourable conditions for the initiation of conservation projects the following measures can be considered:

- The adoption of an appropriate urban development strategy to inform potential investors about and draw their attention to the resources that exist for putting the heritage to use;
- The implementation of a planning and urban development policy that is sufficiently flexible to reconcile the cultural requirements of conservation with the need for projected development to be profitable. This approach can be linked to the adoption of management plans for areas of recognised importance;
- The simplification of administrative procedures such as the need for one form of authorisation;
- The appointment of project co-ordinators and field operators, possibly in the form of a team representing the public and private sector partners, to be fully responsible for a project and capable of overcoming the administrative and financial complexities facing any major conservation project or strategy;
- The preparation of a structured financial evaluation for every maintenance and restoration project, using modern building-site management techniques. This approach can be linked to the use of management plans for single monuments;
- The adoption of a rental policy, where this is a responsibility of the public authorities, that is not a disincentive to private investors.

ii. Intervention measures

Appropriate legal forms should be created to mobilise investors, encourage the reinvestment of profits in new conservation operations or permit the launching of building maintenance and restoration programmes that accord the operator the right to use the building while preserving the rights of the owner. The following examples may be cited:

- Revolving funds using both public and private funds, which with the help of other financial measures will enable either the generation of new money and the automatic renewal of the fund through an original credit mechanism, or the reinvestment of the proceeds in new projects following the sale of completed projects;

- Housing improvement programmes which, combining financial assistance from the state, local authorities and public bodies responsible for social housing, encourage owners to modernise their buildings while guaranteeing low rents;
- A leasing system to enable ownership of a building to be transferred to a specialised company, which would manage and fund the operation and then lease back the restored building to the former owners;
- A 'renovation lease' scheme, the aim of which is to re-market dilapidated housing vacant for that reason, by letting the lessee carry out works and transferring tenure of the building back to the owner after a given period.

iii. Financial measures

There are three principal forms of financial measures:

- *Subsidies (or grant aid)*

The award of grants of money through public subsidy policy should take account of the nature of the operation. Preference may be given to maintenance or restoration of a monument and may depend on other factors such as whether the monument is exclusively used for cultural purposes or for social housing, or is capable of generating a profit. (This may include a group of buildings of historic interest or in an area of cultural significance, whether protected or not). It should also take account of the beneficiaries' income level. With particular reference to social housing, subsidy policy could be designed to encourage the conservation of old buildings rather than the construction of new housing.

- *Loans*

Measures to cover or diminish risks should be taken in order to encourage credit institutions to finance old buildings, particularly by combining mortgage loans with public subsidies, establishing appropriate forms of insurance, and the provision of a public security by a public (particularly local) authority. Diminishing risks can be achieved, for example, by means of a public guarantee. In order to realise their commitment to programmes to enhance the heritage, authorities could also participate in joint structures involving a number of different partners and aimed at handling rehabilitation programmes.

- *Taxation*

Measures should be taken, particularly in countries where the tax system favours investment in new rather than old buildings, to arrive at a situation where taxation provisions encourage maintenance or restoration on old buildings. Different forms of relief can be considered, including income or profits tax, value added tax on the sale of goods and services (including maintenance or restoration works), inheritance tax and land (occupation) taxes.

iv. Specific measures to promote sponsorship

- Measures should be taken to encourage donations (through financial contributions or the donation of assets), not only by means of tax incentives but also by methods likely to promote "popular" sponsorship institutions involving several small businesses or a large number of individuals.
- Specific tax incentives may fall into one or more categories. Measures may be adopted to favour private individuals, by enabling them to claim tax relief on a certain proportion of sums donated for heritage conservation purposes, the proportion varying according to the nature of the beneficiary. Measures may be adopted to relieve firms of company or profit taxes in relation to gratuitous gifts, expenditure to enhance the heritage and expenditure to enable research into architectural heritage. Tax concessions may also be provided to sponsored foundations or non-profit bodies.
- Co-financing procedures could be established to link the award of public loans to the prior collection of private funds from individuals and firms.
- Appropriate legal frameworks should be adopted to enable businesses to make philanthropy part of their management scheme, as a tool of institutional communication. To this end, the advantages traditionally accorded to foundations classed as charitable should be granted to foundations bearing the firm's name whose aim is the maintenance or restoration of part of the heritage. The establishment of specific foundations for the conservation of architectural heritage should be encouraged by the granting of special tax advantages to donors. Encouragement should be given to the establishment of associations of diverse partners for the conservation of the heritage, by recognising their legal status as bodies corporate, their financial autonomy and the appropriate tax advantages.

Furthermore, in recognising that public funds are necessarily limited, the 5th European Conference of Ministers responsible for the cultural heritage (Portorož, 6-7 April 2001) gave further support to encouraging appropriate financial measures and incentives through sponsorship and investment in the less profitable aspects of the heritage.

Moreover, Resolution 1355 (2003) draws attention to Recommendation 1634 (2003) Tax incentives for cultural heritage conservation adopted by the Standing Committee, acting on behalf of the Parliamentary Assembly of the Council of Europe, on 25 November 2003 and the Report of the Committee on Culture, Science and Education under the same title (Doc. 9913 rev.) debated in the Standing Committee, which gave further weight to the idea of encouraging the private sector to invest in architectural heritage through the provision of tax incentives.

1.5. Forms of action and financial assistance

This publication builds on previous work by the Council of Europe, as identified in section 1.4, by providing a more in-depth analysis of measures and examples of systems in operation.

In a number of European countries and also in North America, many different forms of assistance have been developed. Coupled with public-sector-led initiatives, programmes and strategies, a range of mechanisms and practices can be identified and disseminated. These will be examined in the next five chapters of this publication, which consider the following:

- Alternative revenue-raising methods (Chapter 2);
- Grant-aided subsidies (Chapter 3);
- Loan and credit facilities (Chapter 4);
- Fiscal measures (Chapter 5);
- Integrated heritage funding strategies: administration and management (Chapter 6).

2. Alternative revenue-raising methods

2.0. Introduction

Bearing in mind the limitations on state budgets in giving financial support to architectural heritage, a number of other approaches can be identified.

Non-governmental organisations (NGOs), such as heritage trusts, foundations, associations and limited liability companies, can make a significant contribution to raising revenue for built heritage by encouraging private investment, and in some instances may actually administer private and government-backed heritage funding programmes.

The legal regime for the establishment of such bodies will depend on the form of law adopted in particular countries. Countries governed by Common Law (such as the United Kingdom, Ireland and North America) share common legal characteristics, such as a reliance on the court system to provide guidance on the interpretation of law, facilitating the setting up of trusts, associations, charities and non-profit organisations for public benefit. The legal regime governing foundations in Civil Law countries (such as in continental Europe) is not uniform. Foundations are subject to a mixture of private law and public law because they are carriers of private funds dedicated to goals of public interest.

Part IV of the Council of Europe's Recommendation No. R (91) 6 of the Committee of Ministers to member states, on measures likely to promote the funding of the conservation of architectural heritage, gave specific encouragement to the promotion of sponsorship and the establishment and legal recognition of sponsorship organisations, foundations, trusts, charitable organisations and other non-profit legal entities with associated tax advantages (for business and individual donors and for the organisations themselves).

Corporate sponsors can increase their market presence or improve their public image by joining high-profile partnership arrangements and targeting architectural heritage assets that can be developed for commercial purposes.

Economic activity by trusts and foundations and other such bodies in support of their legal purposes should not endanger their character as non-profit bodies. However, all legal systems prohibit such bodies from making payments to the members of their governing bodies or, on liquidation, from distributing assets to such members or to the original founder(s) or predecessors. The majority of countries treat architectural heritage under the "culture" umbrella. Beneficial uses of architectural heritage may incorporate religious, educational or cultural activities. However, considerable differences exist between different countries in the fiscal treatment of charitable bodies. In most countries of the civil law and common law traditions, non-profit organisations and their benefactors enjoy privileged tax treatment, though some countries impose punitive fiscal treatment on charitable bodies.

One can identify a number of types of third sphere (not entirely public or private) organisation for the purpose of raising revenue for architectural heritage.

Chapter 2 also examines methods by which public authorities may raise finance, such as through issuing debt bonds or concession agreements and by applying revenue charges.

In addition, legal tools can be used to secure funding for historic buildings, for example by legal agreements such as easements with associated endowment funds, transferring development rights to safeguard historic buildings with associated legal agreements to ensure funding and by enabling development.

2.1. Charitable trusts

A charitable trust established to safeguard architectural heritage benefits public purposes, which can be treated in law as being charitable. A trust is a relationship, initiated by the settlor, that arises when property is vested in persons called trustees who are obliged to hold such property for the benefit of other persons called beneficiaries. The interest of the beneficiaries will usually be laid down in the instrument creating the trust, but it may be implied or imposed by law. For a trust to be valid, three certainties must be present: certainty of words, certainty of subject and certainty of object.

The income of a charitable trust must be applied exclusively for charitable purposes. While heritage trust organisations around the world vary in emphasis, in general such organisations are charitable (for the benefit of the public), non-profit bodies relying on membership fees, donations of funds and properties, legacies on death, donated skills, tourism revenues, investment incomes and possibly small government donations. Most trust organisations derive additional income from fund-raising and corporate promotion.

The power of trust organisations is granted through legislation. An important power of heritage trust organisations consists of the right to own property inalienably, which means that once declared such property can never be sold or taken from the trust by government except by legislation. Thus, a declaration of inalienability implies perpetual protection of heritage assets donated to charitable trusts. A further legal power is embedded in "conservation agreements" – sometimes termed "restrictive covenants" (see also section 2.5, Easement donations, endowment funds and tax relief) – which can be agreed with owners of privately owned heritage properties who wish to ensure the continuity of their property regardless of future ownership. This legal provision is a continuing burden on the title of the property, regardless of inheritance or succession. This option gives charitable trusts the advantage of perpetually protecting heritage structures without bearing the costs of acquisition, repair or maintenance. In some instances, private donors may retain a lifelong right of personal use or attach conditions to heritage assets donated to the public.

In some countries, trusts can also acquire buildings with the help of allocated government resources, charitable organisations and dedicated lottery revenues. A committed non-government organisation may manage the affairs of a trust in the public interest. This has the added advantage of opening private funding channels that would not be available to government institutions.

The charitable non-profit status of trusts is an important asset in persuading the public to donate money or property. Charitable status may require compliance with government bodies, such as the revenue authorities, or a national charity commission. In most jurisdictions, charitable trusts benefit from fiscal privileges. Examples of charitable trusts can be seen in the United Kingdom and Canada. In both cases, donating income to such bodies has tax benefits.

2.1.1. Example: The National Trust, United Kingdom

The National Trust, established in 1895, is a registered charity charged with the preservation of places of historic interest or natural beauty on behalf of the nation (it covers England, Wales and Northern Ireland; a sister body, the National Trust for Scotland, was established in 1931). It is one of Europe's leading conservation bodies, protecting through ownership, management and covenants over 250 000 hectares of land of outstanding natural beauty and over 1 100 km of coastline.

It cares for over 20 000 heritage buildings and holds protective covenants over many more. These include buildings in vernacular styles and local materials set in rural landscapes, modest dwellings and great houses with associated landscape parks, gardens and temples, ancient monuments, town and industrial buildings, villages and farms. Over 300 historic mansion houses with gardens (many of which hold collections and have fine interiors) are open to the public and in some cases former owners continue to live in properties donated or sold to the Trust. It has a unique legal power to declare land inalienable – such land cannot be sold, mortgaged or compulsorily purchased against the Trust's wishes without special parliamentary procedure. This special power means that protection by the Trust is forever.

The Trust relies on financial support from membership subscriptions (there are over three million members of the National Trust and 270 000 members of the National Trust for Scotland) as well as gifts, legacies and volunteer activity. Because it is a registered charity, membership subscriptions and other donations paid by tax-payers can be increased by 28% at no cost to the donor as the Trust can reclaim the income tax that has already been paid (charities are exempt from tax). Moreover, legacies given to the National Trust are tax-exempt (from inheritance tax). It spends all its income on the care and maintenance of the land and buildings in its protection.

2.1.2. Example: The Architectural Heritage Fund supporting Building Preservation Trusts, United Kingdom

The United Kingdom's Civic Trust first advocated the need for the establishment of Building Preservation Trusts (BPT) in 1968 following a survey of the work of 21 local preservation trusts. In 1971 it observed that many underused and redundant historic buildings could be saved if such trusts had access to working capital and recommended that a

National Building Conservation Fund be established with £1 million in resources. The government endorsed the idea as part of the UK commitment to the Council of Europe campaign for the European Architectural Heritage Year in 1975 by offering up to £500 000 if this could be matched from the private sector.

An appeal was launched and the Architectural Heritage Fund (AHF) was set up in 1976 with a potential revolving fund of £1 million. From the 30 BPTs registered with the AHF in 1976, the number had grown to 270 (with 171 of these working on a revolving fund basis) by 2005 and the accumulated fund of the AHF having grown to £13 million (and has remained around this figure up to 2007). The number of trusts in operation tends to vary from year to year; by 2007 there were a total of 165 BPTs operating in the United Kingdom that were registered with the AHF.

The AHF, a registered charity, promotes the permanent preservation of historic buildings through the provision of financial assistance and advice to BPTs, which are non-profit charitable organisations established to preserve historic buildings for the benefit of the nation. They work on the basis of acquiring protected buildings that are in poor condition or under-occupied or redundant, repairing and rehabilitating them in the public interest and not for profit. As charitable organisations, the AHF and BPTs are able to reclaim income tax on donations and legacies. Every £1 donated qualifies for tax relief and provides £1.28 (as with the National Trust). The 28% rate will reduce to 25% in April 2011 following a government announcement in 2008.

Apart from donations and legacies, the AHF has received financial support from the government, English Heritage (with funding of £129 000 by English Heritage in 2006-7) and other grant-giving bodies. However, a significant amount of its funds comes from the accumulating fund, which provides low-interest loans.

Most BPT projects supported by the AHF involve loans, because most projects need working capital to pay the contractors and professionals while the project is on site, and/or to acquire the building in the first place. Loans are usually essential where the building is being sold after completion. Even if the whole building cost is covered by grants, a loan is often necessary because grant income does not come in when it is needed. Many BPT charities obtain AHF loan offers as a precaution even if they do not expect to need the money. Loans are normally for up to £500 000 and the AHF charges interest at 4% simple rate (rather than compound), payable in one lump sum at the end of the loan period.

The normal loan period is two years, or until the building is sold, which-ever is earlier. For an exceptionally large-scale or complex project, it can be three years. If the building is being sold on completion, the loan is usually repaid from the proceeds. If not, it is repaid from grant income, and/or from longer-term refinancing, usually by mortgaging the building. To protect its charitable funds, the AHF needs security for every loan. This can be either a formal repayment guarantee from a local authority or bank or other acceptable body, or a first charge over property (including the building for which the loan is needed) to which the borrower has a free and marketable title. The amount the AHF can lend will depend upon the value of the security. (See Chapter 4 on Loan and credit facilities.)

The AHF also publishes and annually updates a directory called *Funds for Historic Buildings*. This is a valuable means of identifying possible sources of funds to bridge the conservation gap, including those targeted at other objectives like regeneration, which may nonetheless make the reuse of historic buildings viable.

In addition to its loan facility, the AHF also provides some specific grants to BPTs, including:

- Options Appraisal Grants (which replaced Feasibility Study Grants) to assess the key conservation issues affecting a building and to identify the most viable options in a project likely to qualify for a loan. The grant covers up to 75% of costs of the appraisal, up to a maximum of £7 500 (up to £12 500 in exceptional circumstances such as for complex or large-scale studies);
- Refundable Project Development Grants to help BPTs meet applica-tion requirements of AHF and co-funders (up to £15 000, repayable with interest at 4%). Eligible work may include drawings, specifi-cations, costs, surveys, business plans and conservation plans. The grant may be consolidated into an AHF loan at a later stage;
- Project Organiser Grants to finance project co-ordination by an expe-rienced project manager, either external or a BPT employee (75% of cost up to maximum of £15 000, which is usually spread over more than one year);
- Project Administration Grants providing £4 000 (in four instalments over a 12-month period) towards non-professional costs, including

loan application preparation. This grant is directed towards small trusts with restricted cash-flow. In order to qualify, the BPT must show that it has less than £10 000 in accumulated resources;

There are two main types of BPT that can benefit from these funding measures. Single project trusts, which are formed to tackle a particular building or group of properties, represent about one quarter of all BPTs. They are often set up by members of a local community who are concerned about the condition and future of a particular building. The majority of these trusts, as well as carrying out necessary conservation and rehabilitation work, usually maintain and manage the building when a project has been completed. However, the majority of BPTs work on a revolving fund basis (see section 2.4).

In order to qualify for charitable status (allowing income tax and corporation tax relief), BPTs must register with the United Kingdom's Charity Commission as non-profit organisations. BPTs must obtain consent from the Charity Commission before mortgaging or selling a property, to ensure that the realised sale price is realistic. To ensure the long-term preservation of a building, a BPT may impose restrictive covenants (see also section 2.5 on easement donations, endowment funds and tax relief) requiring the first and successive purchasers to enter into a Deed of Covenant. Alternatively, a BPT may retain the freehold in a building and sell a long lease, ensuring that restrictive covenants can be enforced against a future owner. Charitable status requires the management committee to work for the trust on a voluntary basis. The Trust's Memorandum of Association may allow members to be reimbursed for professional service fees and expenses. Fund-raising activities must be undertaken by setting up a separate trading company that covenants its income to the trust (see section 2.3).

The majority of preservation projects undertaken by BPTs are small-scale and often associated with protected buildings in small towns or rural areas, which may not be priority cases for grant aid or attractive commercial propositions for rehabilitation. The fact that the majority of BPT projects are financially successful provides an exemplar of the approach that could be taken to ensure the survival of many historic buildings at risk (see Figure 1). This approach is backed by United Kingdom Government policy on the historic environment, which specifies that applications for consent to demolish listed buildings must include evidence that the property has been offered for sale at a price that fully considers its state of repair. Moreover, where statutory powers are used to compulsorily acquire buildings in poor condition, it has been recommended that "back-to-back" deals should be organised so that the local authority acquiring a property can immediately resell to a BPT, which can secure the repair and/or rehabilitation of the building and then sell it on to a suitable new owner.

Combined funding of restoration work by a UK charitable trust with limited liability company status

Alderman Fenwick's House was originally a merchant's residence dating from the late 17th century, with 18th-century alterations and additions. In 1781 it became a coaching inn and then in 1883 it became a political club. In 1962, the building was vacated and fell into a state of disrepair.

In 1974 Newcastle City Council was required to buy the building, on the basis of a legal argument that the building was incapable of "reasonably beneficial use" following refusal of permission to demolish the listed building. The City Council later offered Tyne and Wear Building Preservation Trust the opportunity to take over and restore the building with a £100 000 start-up project grant, of which £60 000 went on professional fees to cover the cost of an initial structural survey (including archaeological analysis) and a feasibility study. In 1982 the building was acquired by the Trust on a 125-year lease, with the first 25 years rent-free and an annual rent of £2 500 thereafter.

The first three restoration phases concentrated on the fabric, to ensure protection from external elements, with a new roof, windows, brickwork and rainwater goods, and were completed by 1992 at a cost of about £560 000. Most of the funds for this work came from grant aid provided by the City Council and English Heritage. The remainder was financed by private charitable trusts, private donations and fund-raising activities.

In 1992 Tyne and Wear BPT decided to proceed with a final phase of work, but at first had difficulty in securing the required funds. By 1995, 100% grant funding was secured for the remaining works: £600 000 from the European Regional Development Fund as an employment creation project, £300 000 from English Heritage and £750 000 from the Heritage Lottery Fund. The Architectural Heritage Fund provided a loan of £300 000 to the trust to ease cash-flow problems (due to delays in receiving grants). Work began on site in 1995 and was completed in 1997 (an 18-month contract).

The Trust originally expected to sell the building, to clear any remaining debts, but on completion and having received 100% grant aid, it decided to retain the long leasehold interest to provide rental income. The annual rent pays for the salary of the manager of the Building Preservation Trust, feasibility studies for other trust projects, insurance costs on buildings held by the trust and a nominal internal debt (as the project had to borrow from the trust's capital reserves).

Figure 1 – Alderman Fenwick's House, Newcastle upon Tyne, England

This historic building was restored and rehabilitated by the Tyne and Wear Building Preservation Trust Limited, helped by funding from many sources.

2.1.3. Example: Heritage Canada Foundation

Canada has a variety of heritage organisations, foundations and non-profit bodies registered as charitable trusts. Charitable tax receipts are provided for donations so that donors can reclaim tax on the amount donated. At federal level, the Heritage Canada Foundation was created by the federal government as a non-governmental charity in 1973; at the provincial level there are various similar charitable trust heritage organisations.

The Heritage Canada Foundation was granted an endowment by the federal government to ensure that it would remain financially, administratively and politically independent. The foundation has operated specific support schemes, including an area conservation programme (to assist in the adaptive reuse of heritage buildings within an area), a property programme (including the acquisition of properties for the purpose of creating joint ventures for their restoration), a "main street" programme (to help revitalise the centres of small and medium-sized towns) and a heritage regions programme (to help regenerate rural areas).

The present focus of the foundation is, however, on acting as a national advocate in key areas such as tax reform and heritage policy, promoting awareness of national heritage issues such as working with municipalities to recognise and use heritage properties and amenities for the benefit of communities, and conducting research and disseminating findings in the field of heritage conservation. The foundation has Crown trustee status so that it can offer tax incentives to encourage the donation of real or personal property in support of its aims and objectives. It is custodian of five heritage properties.

2.1.4. Example: Ontario Heritage Trust, Canada

Ontario Heritage Trust (Foundation until 2005) has operated for over forty years and is the lead heritage agency for the province of Ontario. It is a Crown Agency with charitable trust status, reporting to the Minister of Culture of the province. Its principal activities are to promote the importance of heritage conservation; preserve and protect significant heritage sites; uphold and advocate the highest standards of conservation; demonstrate the adaptive reuse of heritage properties; commemorate important heritage sites and events with plaques; encourage community heritage activities and the involvement of young people in heritage activities; and to raise revenue to support heritage activities. As a charitable trust, it benefits from tax relief on all gifts of money and the fully appraised value of gifts of property and heritage conservation easements (see also section 2.5). The foundation's properties held in trust include 24 built heritage sites (11 of which have been designated as National Heritage Sites) and 140 natural heritage properties. It also holds, in trust, over 650 000 archaeological artefacts related to its properties and the title to about 200 conservation easement agreements.

With financial assistance from the provincial government and donations from the private sector and individuals, the foundation has undertaken extensive conservation work on the properties it holds in trust and their associated collections. Finance is also raised through income from properties held in trust, the rental of properties for conferences, offices or film locations, the sale of heritage-related merchandise, public tours of some sites, and the interest earned on investment funds and other sources.

2.2. Heritage foundations

Heritage foundations fulfil various functions in the conservation of architectural heritage. They are registered in public records, and the courts exercise jurisdiction where foundations fail or violate the law. Foundations are considered legal persons that can participate in civil life in the same way as natural persons.

Heritage assets can be entrusted to foundations on the basis that a building or site will only be used for a specified purpose in keeping with its cultural heritage importance. Apart from giving grants, foundations can promote financial support for architectural heritage through fund-raising campaigns. National laws differ on the permissible purposes of foundations, varying between complete liberty for the founders to decide the purpose (Netherlands law simply requires a "given purpose") to a strict determination of purposes by the law. Fiscal legislation on the deductibility of charitable donations may include allowances for direct donations to heritage assets in addition to donations to foundations (see section 5.6).

Legislation in some civil law countries, including Belgium, France and Germany, requires foundations to obtain prior consent or participation of a state body. In Denmark and the Netherlands, registration is required only for certain types of foundation, and the possession of legal personality does not depend on registration. Some countries require a minimum initial capital as a precondition for the existence of a foundation.

2.2.1. Foundations in France

French law distinguishes three types of foundation:
- A public utility foundation (*fondation reconnue d'utilité publique*) – one that is recognised as having a public use – cannot be created unless it has undergone a procedure that has been validated by the Conseil d'Etat, which is France's highest administrative court.
- A sheltered foundation (*fondation arbritée* or *sous égide*) does not have separate legal status, but works through another foundation that is willing and able to shelter it.

- A corporate foundation (*fondation d'enterprise*) has a more flexible legal regime.

Where cultural heritage is concerned, three different categories of foundation come into play:
- bodies that distribute money for various purposes,
- bodies that specialise in heritage conservation, and
- bodies that focus on one building or site.

Firstly, there are foundations that distribute money for general purposes. They can finance restoration, conservation and enhancement either directly or through sheltered foundations.

The Fondation de France, created in 1969, is such an umbrella organisation. It can assist individuals, businesses and associations in carrying out projects of a generally philanthropic, social, cultural or environmental nature or in health-related matters. It is an autonomous, non-political entity governed by private law, but also a non-profit organisation. The Fondation de France has three main objectives: to collect funds for various purposes, including cultural and environmental projects; to assist in developing and running associations; and to encourage private sponsorship. It acts as a framework within which foundations can be established, and many firms and private individuals have established cultural foundations under the aegis of the Fondation de France.

Secondly, there are institutions or foundations that specialise in preserving and enhancing heritage, which is the case for the Fondation du Patrimoine ('Heritage Foundation'), which was created by legislation in 1996 and given public utility status in 1997. The goal of this heritage foundation is to preserve, develop and spread awareness of the national heritage, focusing in particular on the identification, preservation and restoration of unprotected rural and vernacular heritage. It supports the upkeep of monuments, individual buildings and groups of buildings, and natural or landscaped areas of interest that are threatened by decay, degradation or ruin, and it also provides employment and training in restoration and heritage preservation work. It is the only organisation in France authorised by the Ministry of Economy and Finance to issue a "label" to sites of cultural interest; this allows a tax deduction for maintenance and restoration work on buildings not protected by the state. The Fondation du Patrimoine also benefits from an allocation of revenue from the state, which has been collected from a fraction of inheritance tax.

Since legislation in 2003 the awarding of a label (for a period of five years) has resulted in certain private landowners being immediately eligible to receive tax deductions. Eligible beneficiaries include private landowners or individuals who are liable to income tax and groups of private individuals in co-ownership of property. The tax deduction can be given for buildings visible from public thoroughfares that are not used for business purposes in the following categories:

- Uninhabitable properties that are part of local heritage, in both rural and urban areas (such as dovecots, wash houses, bread ovens, chapels and windmills);
- Habitable or non-habitable properties that are typical of the rural heritage (including small farms, barns, village properties and small country houses). While these types of buildings are mostly located in rural areas some buildings now in urban areas (following expansion of built-up areas) are also eligible to receive the Label.
- Habitable or non-habitable properties situated in a zone of architectural, urban and landscape importance (ZZAUP) (see also section 5.2.3).

Eligible work includes high-quality work on a building's exterior, that has been approved by the Official Architect (Architecte des Bâtiments de France) and aims to preserve the original character of the building. For uninhabitable buildings, work on the interior may be carried out if the owner agrees to open the building to the public. With the Label of the Fondation du Patrimoine, owners can obtain a tax deduction for the cost of approved works against their net taxable revenue, if the building does not generate income, and against property tax subject to certain limits.

Foundations of the third type contribute to conserving and enhancing a structure or particular site. They can be corporate foundations that are recognised as having a public role.

The system of corporate foundations (fondations d'entreprise) was established by legislation in 1991, modified in 2002, to encourage commercial bodies to sponsor culture, specifically heritage, and to lend continuity to their sponsorship activities. A corporate foundation is a legal entity established by a company to carry out, for profit, work in the public interest that cannot be funded through donations, bequests or appeals to the generosity of the public. The possibility of working for gain makes this a better solution for businesses as compared to public interest foundations of a more general nature. However, in return the foundation must provide for a programme of grants of a defined value over several years, as well as an initial endowment calculated in proportion to the amount of the grant programme, being between one fifth of the minimum total value of grants and one fifth of the actual programme amount. Corporate foundations may receive public subsidies from local or regional authorities.

In the majority of cases these three categories of foundation support restoration projects and help to manage a monument, architectural ensemble or site; it is very rare for them to be the owners of such heritage assets (see further: section 5.6.3).

2.2.2. Foundations in Belgium

An annual subsidy is provided though the budget of the Flemish Regional Administration of Belgium for non-profit organisations that fulfil tasks complementary to the management of architectural heritage. As an example of a foundation operating in Belgium, the Flemish Foundation of Monuments and Sites (Stichting Vlaams Erfgved) can be cited. This is a non-profit organisation that has been in operation since 1993. Foundation members, totalling over 3 000, are entitled to tax relief on membership fees and donations. The foundation also receives regional funding to cover administration costs and restoration projects. It holds a number of government and non-government monuments. To avoid complex administrative procedures, architectural monuments owned by the regional government may be transferred to the foundation for a nominal sum. The restoration and future management of the monument, including public access, then become the responsibility of the foundation.

2.2.3. Foundations in the Netherlands

There are two types of organisation working as non-profit agencies in the field of monument preservation in the Netherlands. Most operate in the form of a limited liability company (see section 2.3), while others operate more as a society or association but resemble a foundation in terms of tax incentives and sponsorship.

The Dutch Preservation Society Hendrick de Keyser is an example of such an organisation. Hendrick de Keyser was set up in 1918 as an idealistic society depending on donations of money from members and the donation of historic houses. The objective of the society is non-profit-making activity to preserve architecturally or historically important buildings. Its members' donations, typically from €50 to €500 per annum, are invested in society restoration projects. All proceeds are re-invested in restoration and maintenance projects. Hendrick de Keyser is unique among preservation organisations in the Netherlands because it guarantees the continued integrity of the building in an authentic condition both internally and externally. Owners place historic monuments in the ownership of the society to ensure sympathetic restoration and maintenance in perpetuity. Over 300 historic properties have been consigned to the care of Hendrick de Keyser, across 64 municipalities in the Netherlands, with over 100 of these being donated.

Property held by the society is never sold, but may be let out to tenants. If the original use of the monument cannot be maintained, the society strives to find a new use similar to the historical one. Where possible, the society also ensures that the original layout is maintained. From the rental income of let properties that have been restored, the society uses 20% to finance administration and staff wages, another 40% to pay for maintenance and a further 40% to finance restoration projects and buy monuments.

As a non-profit entity, the society is exempt from income tax. Tax relief against income and corporation tax is also available on donations to the society (subject to certain limits). The society must pay inheritance tax on gifts over a defined value, but at a reduced rate of 11% (instead of 30%) based on its non-profit status.

The society also receives state subsidies for restoration work on the historic fabric of monuments. Generally 60% of the costs are eligible for subsidy at a rate of 70%, resulting in a subsidy of about 42% of the total costs (see section 3.3.6). Because the society is registered as an "idealistic foundation" and is a non-profit organisation, exempt from paying income or corporation tax, it is entitled to an increased subsidy of 70% on eligible restoration works. Private individuals and companies receive a 20% subsidy on eligible works but, unlike the society, may supplement this with income/corporation tax relief.

The society may also borrow money from a bank or from the National Restoration Fund, but it must pay market interest rates. However, financial institutions are positively disposed to lend money to the society based on its perceived security.

2.2.4. Foundations in Germany

The establishment of foundations in Germany requires the permission of the Foundation Regulatory Authority (*Stiftungsaufischt*) in the federal state where the organisation is based. The charitable or philanthropic status of such institutions is determined under German Excise Law (*Abgabenordnung*). These tax regulations specify that such institutions will be freed from corporation (profit) tax, trade tax and land tax (but not purchase tax on property) if their purpose is exclusively to serve the general welfare in a material, cultural or moral sense. The relevant state finance ministry determines the level of tax reduction applicable. Donations to foundations are usually given relief at 5% on income tax, but where the purpose of the foundation is cultural the relief is 10%.

Public and private foundations can play a significant role in financing architectural heritage conservation projects in Germany. For example, in the public sector, the Baden-Württemberg Heritage Foundation (Denkmalstiftung Baden-Württemberg), set up in 1985, finances architectural heritage conservation projects by private individuals, heritage action groups, municipalities and churches, and the North-Rhine-Westphalia Heritage Foundation (Nordrhein-Westfalen-Stiftung Naturschutz, Heimat und Kulturpflege) was established in 1986 to promote natural and cultural monuments. Examples of private-sector foundations include the Wustenrot Foundation (Stiftung Wustenrot), which was set up in 1990 to support the preservation of architectural monuments in the eastern states of Germany (extending its remit to western states in Germany in 2002), and the Messerschmidt Foundation (Messerschmidt Stiftung), established by the founder of the aviation company, which changed its original dedication from problems in the field of aeronautics and astronautics to the "maintenance and preservation of German artistic and cultural monuments at home and abroad".

2.2.5. Example: The National Foundation
for Architectural Heritage Protection
(Deutsche Stiftung Denkmalschutz: DSD)

DSD was established in 1985 as a private trust with an initial capital of 500 000 deutschmark (about €250 000) donated by 23 well-known companies to support the preservation and restoration of important cultural monuments. The foundation supports requests for assistance from monument owners and smaller specific building foundations, such as for churches or castles (DSD has helped to set up over 100 non-profit foundations). The aim of the foundation is to preserve endangered cultural monuments and to promote the idea of monument care through long-term maintenance and preservation (including their rehabilitation to new uses if carried out in a sensitive manner).

It sets strict criteria for projects, requiring that its limited funds generate the greatest impact, by concentrating on endangered monuments where action is not sufficiently guaranteed by government aid or where DSD funding could help lever other public funds. Social considerations may also be taken into account, such as the rehabilitation of protected buildings for community facilities, churches or for young people that the foundation chooses to assist, particularly in areas where help is most needed. Support is not only for the buildings, but also for the people behind these buildings. The foundation manages private rehabilitation initiatives with cultural heritage and social aspects, such as providing employment.

The foundation has a large capital fund comprising capital assets (such as land, buildings and investments) and other assets including book stocks, publishing products and a cash fund. It raises some of its funds from private individuals and companies who benefit from a provision allowing 10% tax relief on donations to cultural institutions. Over 170 000 private donors and companies have donated to the foundation over its lifetime (amounting to over €120 million). Since 1991 it has received part of its income from the Glucks-Spirale television lottery (DSD receives one third, and the other two thirds go to sport and social welfare) with €18 million provided from this source during 2004. It also receives occasional contributions from the federal government (over €3 million in 2004). These sources have enabled the foundation to provide over €390 million in funding to endangered heritage in Germany for some 3 200 projects.

The foundation looks after many church buildings and monuments, such as castles and small palaces owned by municipal authorities, mostly in eastern Germany. Since reunification, the DSD foundation has focused its funding on the eastern states. Under the agreement for the reunification of Germany, property confiscated by the communist government was not returned to the original owners following reunification, but placed in the ownership of municipal governments (communities). Many of these monuments were left in poor condition and the municipal authorities lacked the financial resources to repair and maintain them.

2.3. Limited liability companies

Various legal systems have different types of incorporation, but all jurisdictions have a corporate body equivalent to a company with broadly similar characteristics. Most jurisdictions distinguish between public and private companies. Companies limited by guarantee are the most common for architectural heritage conservation purposes in the United Kingdom, rather than companies limited by shares (but special arrangements can be made for companies working in the field of building preservation, as in the Netherlands or Germany).

In United Kingdom law a company limited by shares is used for investment purposes and commercial ventures. The liability of shareholders to meet the debts of a company is limited to the amount paid for the shares at the outset. On the other hand, in a company limited by guarantee the members do not pay any money unless and until the company is unable to pay its debts. Members agree to guarantee the company's debts up to a certain sum (which is usually a nominal sum) in the event of dissolution. Limited liability by guarantee is an attractive vehicle for use in the conservation of the architectural heritage as creditors of the company are unable, should the assets of the company be insufficient, to look to the shareholders to make good any shortfall.

2.3.1. Example: Building Preservation Trusts

The model of a company limited by guarantee is often used for Building Preservation Trusts (BPTs) (see section 2.1.2). Thus interested persons can establish such a trust without incurring personal financial risk. Although BPTs are voluntary charitable organisations, in order to protect trust members from being personally responsible if a BPT falls into financial difficulties, they are normally incorporated with limited liability provisions as a company limited by guarantee. This requires the establishment of a management committee (the equivalent to a Board of Directors in company law), which is responsible for the general control, administration and management of the BPT as a charity. The members of the management committee effectively act as charity trustees and are required to appoint a company secretary who is responsible for the BPT's accounts, which must be filed annually with the Registrar of Companies. As a charitable trust, the company benefits from tax relief.

Generally, the underlying principles of a company (ownership and profit) conflict with the principles of a charitable trust (protecting heritage assets for public benefit). But a BPT incorporated as a company limited by guarantee is essentially a not-for-profit company. If a company goes into liquidation, heritage assets may be sold for the benefit of the creditors.

Different models are operated in other countries. For example, companies in the Netherlands for the purpose of assisting the architectural heritage can be established as limited liability companies but with shareholders.

2.3.2. Example: Stadsherstel Amsterdam NV (The Amsterdam Restoration Company)

The threat of comprehensive redevelopment in Amsterdam in the 1950s led to action to save historic buildings. A group of businessmen founded a limited liability company (Naamloze Vennootschap) in 1956 for this purpose and approached important Amsterdam companies to join the venture, which was independent of the city council. The capital of the company came from the shareholders, including communities, businesses and banks based in Amsterdam. In 1957, Stadsherstel Amstel (the Company for City Restoration) obtained the legal status of a public housing corporation, entailing tax advantages such as exemption from company tax (35% of profit) and property transfer duties (paid on the purchase price). In 1970, the City of Amsterdam became a shareholder. The company concentrated on buying and rehabilitating threatened historic buildings, mainly protected monuments, returning historic houses to residential use with modern interiors and maintaining the buildings they owned.

The Amsterdam Monumenten Fonds NV was founded in 1992, to restore 19th-century listed monuments such as churches that could not be adapted to residential or commercial use without damage to the building interior. Many shareholders of Stadsherstel Amstel became shareholders of this new company and in 1999 the two companies consolidated their organisations, following negotiations with the ministries of Housing and Culture, the city authorities and the shareholders. As a result, Stadsherstel Amsterdam NV now restores all types of threatened monuments, not just dwellings (see Figure 2).

Stadsherstel Amsterdam NV (The Amsterdam Restoration Company) has achieved the synthesis of a private profit-making limited company and an institution serving the common good through public-private partnership in restoring and rehabilitating buildings in the city of Amsterdam. It is essentially a non-profit making organisation that operates as a revolving fund (See section 2.4). The contradictory nature of a profit-making limited liability company and a non-profit public housing corporation is justified by the fact that the annual dividend to shareholders is fixed at 5% (and commercial share-holders are exempt from tax on this income so long as the upgraded value of a building does not exceed the cost of works). The low dividend ensures that shareholders invest in the company for social reasons. In the case of dissolution, the shareholders only receive their initial capital outlay plus the dividend on it. Any surplus funds go to the Central Fund for Public Housing or to an institution for restoring historic monuments. Limited companies of this nature are also exempt from paying VAT on work carried out on properties that are rehabilitated for commercial use, as opposed to residential use. Stadsherstel Amsterdam NV often operates by restoring monumental features of protected historic houses and then sub-dividing them into apartments, sometimes with a commercial – office or retail – use on the ground floor (see Figure 3).

Shareholders' capital has been used by the company to buy prop-erties. After over 50 years' work, funding for projects now mainly comes from rental income from properties held by the company which have been restored and rehabilitated (by the end of 2001 the company owned 453 buildings). The company generally retains ownership of its properties in perpetuity to ensure continued main-tenance, with about 20% of rental income being used to maintain properties over a four-year programme. Occasionally properties held by the company may be sold to raise a large capital sum to assist in paying for a major project. Subsidies for work on historic buildings have also been obtained, but the company has relied less on this source of funding in recent years.

There are about forty similar organisations working on monuments in the Netherlands. Stadsherstal has equivalent companies based elsewhere, such as Stadsherstel Hague, but all these limited liability companies are separate. They meet once a year to discuss issues of common interest.

A limited liability restoration company: Stadsherstel Amsterdam NV

Figure 2 – The Amstelkerk, built between 1668 and 1670

This was originally a temporary church for inhabitants in the new belt formed by the canals around Amsterdam's city centre. Stadsherstel Amsterdam NV acquired the building in 1986, when it was in poor condition, began restoration work in 1990 and set up its office in part of the building in 1991. The nave is available to let in the evenings and at weekends for lectures, conferences, concerts, dinners and receptions.

Figure 3 – Historic canal houses in Kerkstraat, Amsterdam

Stadsherstel Amsterdam NV has restored and rehabilitated many of these typical buildings as apartments or for mixed commercial and residential use, including nos. 323, 328 and 329-331 Kerkstraat.

2.3.3. Example: Brandenburgische Schlösser GmbH

Non-profit foundations for architectural heritage in Germany have difficulty in setting up a revolving fund to purchase and restore buildings because they would incur a tax liability if any profit was made on the sale of the property above a defined limit (about €30 000 per annum) and this could result in the organisation losing its tax-efficient status as a foundation. To avoid this situation a form of limited liability company can be used for private-sector activity (and sponsorship) in the field of monument preservation – known as a *Gemeinnützige Betriesbsgellschaft* (GmbH), a non-profit-holding company for community benefit. Such a company has members called partners, who by law can only be held liable for a specified sum of the capital invested. This arrangement is similar to the way the Architectural Heritage Fund supports Building Preservation Trusts in the United Kingdom.

In 1992, the German National Foundation for the Protection of Monuments (Deutsche Stiftung Denkmalshutz: DSD) formed such a non-profit-holding company in partnership with the federal state of Brandenburg (including the City of Berlin), called the Brandenburgische Schlösser GmbH. The company operates by taking over under-used heritage properties owned by towns and municipalities, particularly large buildings such as castles of local importance, and by investing annual grants from the DSD foundation and the state (Land Brandenburg) for sensitive restoration with a view to finding new users. The DSD foundation provided funding of €4.5 million in 2007.

Under German law, by this arrangement the municipality (community) retains ownership of the monument in the long term, but the restoration project and letting rights belong to the company (the right to hold such properties is usually gained by payment of a nominal sum, typically €1). The municipality can only take full ownership rights back from the company if the partners agree. As a result, the company cannot sell the restored monument following restoration, but can rent the building to new users and the rental income is used to fund future projects. The rent level is usually below a market rent to ensure that there is new use of the property and therefore an income stream to ensure that future maintenance can be guaranteed. In the future, it is envisaged that the company will become financially self-sufficient with the rental from restored buildings. The method of managing projects prior to finding a new user provides the company with strong bargaining power to negotiate strict guidelines with new occupants over future management and maintenance plans to protect heritage monuments.

The Brandenburgische Schlösser GmbH has been successful in managing the restoration and rehabilitation of a small number of castles and palaces. By the end of 2007, sixteen properties had been repaired and a further five rehabilitated for a new use.

2.4. Revolving funds

A revolving fund provides a proactive tool for heritage conservation organisations to buy endangered properties and resell them to sympathetic buyers with protective covenants. The principle of revolving funds is that capital investment in one property is recovered (or even enhanced by some return on capital) through sale or letting of the improved building, so the money can be recycled into improvements to a further property. A revolving fund is therefore a pool of capital created and reserved for a specific activity such as heritage conservation, with the restriction that the monies are returned to the fund to be reused for similar activities.

The most common source of start-up capital for revolving funds is grant aid from local foundations, corporations or state or local government agencies. As funds gradually become depleted, fund-raising is a continual activity of most revolving funds. To attract capital from donors, a privately operated revolving fund should be incorporated as a non-profit, tax-exempt organisation. To retain tax-exempt status, a revolving fund must be organised and operated exclusively for exempt purposes and no part of its net earnings may add to the benefit of any private shareholders or individual. Local lending institutions can provide funding in the form of a line of credit secured by the fund's assets or personal guarantees. When a property needs emergency stabilisation or when the size of the conservation task is a deterrent to buyers, funds may carry out necessary works prior to resale, acting as a developer of last resort. Revolving funds can also lend money to enable sympathetic buyers to acquire and repair historic properties.

A variety of public or private entities can operate a revolving fund, but the majority of funds that buy and sell properties are managed by private, non-profit organisations. Non-profit heritage conservation revolving funds rely on techniques such as rehabilitation agreements and restrictive covenants to ensure the appropriate repair work and long-term protection of the properties they assist. Remedies in the event of non-conformance must be included in the agreement, such as the right to sue for specific performance, provision for liquidated damages or the right of the fund to complete the rehabilitation and place a lien on the property for the expenditure incurred.

Revolving funds are most effective when they target areas or properties that have been neglected by the private sector. Some funds are reactive, waiting for potential properties to come to them, whereas some funds are proactive, instigating area-based heritage projects. Properties sold to revolving funds at less than fair market value are termed bargain sales, where the vendor benefits from a charitable contribution deduction for the difference between the bargain sale price and the market value of the property.

2.4.1. Example: The Architectural Heritage Fund and Building Preservation Trusts

The United Kingdom's Architectural Heritage Fund (see section 2.1.2) effectively works as a revolving fund. Over a 30-year period the fund has risen from £1 million to £13 million. Up to 2005 the AHF had offered grants totalling over £4 million and loans of more than £82 000 million from this accumulating fund.

The majority of Building Preservation Trusts (BPTs; see section 2.1.2) carry out multiple projects in their lifetime, in a particular geographical area such as a town or city, and some concentrate on particular types of building and operate on a revolving fund basis by acquiring, restoring/rehabilitating and disposing of buildings. Any development surplus derived from sale proceeds, less any loan repayment, is used as working capital towards the next project. (Note that this surplus is not profit, as a BPT is working for the charitable purpose of saving historic buildings in the public interest.) Loans from the AHF are usually short-term, depending on the time taken to complete the project and dispose of the building. During periods of market recession, BPTs may choose to retain ownership and let properties (providing income) until the capital values increase or they may retain ownership of historic buildings to use as security for loans for further projects.

2.4.2. Example: Nationaal Restauratiefonds, Netherlands

A National Restoration Fund (NRF) was established in the Netherlands in 1985, because of a shortage of funds to subsidise protected monuments: at the time there was a long wait for the determination of applications for subsidies and also for their payment, which obstructed the progress in restoring monuments.

The government decided to use an existing private-sector organisation to run this fund, namely Bouwfonds, a large company specialising in property development, management and finance, including the provision of home and investment mortgages and project financing. However, the organisation has a close relationship with national and local authorities because its shareholders are all local government municipalities, and the ministry dealing with cultural affairs maintains control over what the NRF can do. Bouwfonds receives a management fee for running the fund which, in turn, has its own board of governors.

The government provided the fund with a loan of 5 million guilders when it began. The fund is essentially a revolving fund and one of its first requirements was to repay the loan once the resources of the fund had built up. However, the fund has been replenished, not just by loan repayments but by further grants from the Ministry of Finance under a strategic plan for the care of monuments until 2010. The agreement to pay these additional amounts to the NRF arose from studies that showed that public investment in heritage resulted in an 8% rise in tax payments resulting from work carried out for monument care and restoration.

The NRF provides two services for owners of protected monuments. Firstly, it provides advice to owners to assist them in financing management projects. This includes information about appropriate architects and contractors, though without specific recommendations – addresses are given for specialist restoration architects and contractors, from which the owner can choose. Secondly, the NRF manages the subsidy programme provided by the government, and provides pre-financing schemes for subsidised work and "restoration mortgages".

Grant-aid subsidy awards are made according to predetermined amounts allocated to provincial and municipal authorities in four-year programmes, and different levels of award (by percentage of costs) are made, depending on the type of property and whether the owner of a monument is a taxpayer or not (see section 3.3.6).

A subsidy award is only paid once the work for an approved scheme has been completed. Due to this the NRF provides a pre-financing scheme to cover the cost of works while they are being carried out. This advanced financing prevents further deterioration of monuments and allows economies to be made on, for example, the increase in prices of materials and labour costs that would occur, and allows a monument to be ready for use as soon as possible.

In addition, the NRF has provided loans in the form of "restoration mortgages" since 1990 (see section 4.2, The Netherlands). These are low-interest (subsidised) loans. The rate is fixed for the period of the loan and is usually set at 5% less than the normal bank loan rate (and has been set as low as 1%). The loans usually last for 30 years, but can be paid back earlier without penalty. The revolving fund is fed by instalments of interest on loans plus other business revenues of the NRF, including loan redemptions, so that other monument owners can be assisted in the future.

2.4.3. Revolving funds in the USA

There are many revolving funds operating in the USA. The National Trust for Historic Preservation plays a significant role, by operating two revolving funds itself and assisting other organisations to establish revolving funds.

The National Trust for Historic Preservation was created in 1949. It finances its work through its members and the contributions of individuals, corporations and foundations. Though the National Historic Preservation Act of 1966 provided federal funding for the trust's work, this appropriation was terminated by mutual agreement in 1998. Since then the trust has relied on private-sector contributions. Donations can benefit from tax relief, and the gift of heritage property avoids capital gains tax on the property's appreciated value and provides a charitable tax deduction from federal income tax.

It operates the National Trust Loan Fund, which has a 30-year track record of lending to low-income historic districts and to specific endangered historic resources. It consists of two preservation revolving funds: the Inner-City Ventures Fund and the National Preservation Loan Fund.

The combined asset base of these funds has grown since 1994 from some $4 million to about $10 million.

The Inner-City Ventures Fund provides low-interest loans to organisations for projects that re-use designated historic properties for affordable housing, community facilities, retail and office space in low- and mixed-income neighbourhoods. The loan rate is usually fixed at 1% below normal bank loan rate.

The National Preservation Loan Fund is more flexible in its project criteria, funding a variety of preservation projects at below market rate. These include establishing or expanding specific local and state-wide preservation revolving funds, acquiring and/or rehabilitating historic buildings, sites, structures and districts, and preserving National Historic Landmarks. Eligible applicants are tax-exempt non-profit organisations; local, state, or regional governments; and for-profit organisations. Preference is given to non-profit and public-sector organisations.

Properties eligible for loans are local, state or nationally designated historic resources; contributing resources in a certified local, state or national historic district; resources eligible for listing on a local, state, or national register; or locally recognised historic resources. The loan amount is based on the type of project and use of funds, with a maximum loan amount of $350 000 and loan terms ranging from one to seven years. Projects must comply with the Secretary of the Interior's Standards for the Treatment of Historic Properties.

Other examples of revolving funds include the state-based revolving fund operated by Preservation North Carolina and the City of New York's Landmarks Conservancy Historic Properties Fund.

2.4.4. Example: Preservation North Carolina

Preservation North Carolina (PNC) was founded in 1939 and is the state of North Carolina's only private, non-profit, state-wide historic preservation organisation. Its mission is to protect and promote buildings, landscapes and sites important to the heritage of North Carolina. In 1975, the North Carolina Society for the Preservation of Antiquities (now PNC) received $35 000 from the Mary Babcock Reynolds Foundation to create a small revolving fund to acquire endangered historic structures (starting in 1977). Since this time the revolving fund has developed and enjoys a national reputation, having been cited by the National Park Service as "the premier state-wide preservation organisation of the South, if not the Nation" and the National Trust for Historic Preservation as "the model organisation of its kind".

Through its award-winning Endangered Properties Program, PNC acquires endangered historic properties and then finds buyers willing and able to rehabilitate them. It has helped save over 500 endangered properties, levering an estimated $100 million in private investment. PNC has a net worth of more than $5 million and is supported by over 4 000 members.

In 80% of the cases, Preservation North Carolina secures an option to purchase property at a given price over a fixed period. During this option period, usually ranging from three months to two years, PNC markets the property and secures a buyer who is willing to acquire the property subject to protective covenants. Since the charitable purpose of PNC is to resell property, the property held for resale is exempt from property tax. Alternatively, the revolving fund secures funds to directly purchase property, sometimes at a price less than market value. Occasionally properties are donated as a gift to PNC. It may also take a long-term lease on a property in order to protect it.

The significant aspect of the PNC's revolving fund is the relatively modest amount of money that is required to run the programme each year (about $500 000). Despite this, it is usually working at any given time with more than $5 million in property.

Local, city and county governments and school districts receive over $1 million every year from the property tax revenues generated by the buildings with which PNC has been involved. The impact of the revolving fund is increased by the fact that prospective purchasers seek to buy and rehabilitate property in close proximity to revolving fund properties.

2.4.5. Example: New York Landmarks Conservancy Historic Properties Fund

The New York Landmarks Conservancy (NYLC) has since 1982 operated a revolving loan fund known as the Historic Properties Fund, whose purpose is to offer low-interest loans, grants and technical assistance to owners of historic residential, non-profit, religious and commercial properties throughout the city, mostly in low- to moderate-income communities. Since 1982 the Historic Properties Fund has assisted over 200 buildings, awarding more than $14 million in loans and over $300 000 in grants. The fund is one of the largest private revolving loan funds in the USA that is used exclusively for historic preservation action.

Loans are generally provided for exterior work or for structural repairs, and range from $20 000 to $300 000. Interest rates are generally below market rates, and loan terms are usually up to 10 years. There is a requirement that a loan must be secured through a first or second mortgage or other acceptable collateral.

Eligible recipients of loans are owners of individually designated historic landmark properties, properties in certified historic districts, or buildings listed or eligible for listing in the State or National Register of Historic Places within one of the five boroughs of New York City.

The Landmark Conservancy's professional staff and consulting archi-tects work with every loan recipient to manage the process of restoring older buildings. They assist in developing plans and specifications, select qualified contractors, negotiate bids, obtain any necessary approvals and permits, and ensure that the work is performed correctly.

2.5. Easement donations, endowment funds and tax relief

Legislatures can stimulate the architectural heritage policies they desire by defining property rights in ways that encourage efficient and socially desirable private-sector transactions involving heritage prop-erty. One such way is through the use of preservation (or conservation) easements, as used in the United States and Canada.

An easement is a legal agreement designed to ensure long-term pres-ervation of architectural heritage by prohibiting demolition or inap-propriate alterations. Preservation easements, also called "restrictive covenants", are in practice used to safeguard facades, interior features and even views. Easements originate in common law (as developed in the United Kingdom, Commonwealth countries and North America) and have evolved through court decisions involving immovable prop-erty and contracts.

Easement agreements work on the basis that the owner of a historic structure donates a preservation easement to a non-profit preservation organisation or government entity while maintaining private ownership. By the agreement, the owner forfeits certain rights (such as to be able to sub-divide or develop the property for commercial activity) and it may compel the owner to maintain or restore the property. In fact, an easement agreement may authorise the receiving organisation to make repairs or correct violations at the owner's expense. Such an agreement is enforceable through the courts.

Preservation easement donations may apply for a term of years or in perpetuity. The easement applies to the land and binds future property owners to its provisions, in many cases providing stronger protection than heritage designation.

Most easement programmes require the easement donor to contribute to an "easement endowment" or administration fund, which is used to cover the cost of annual inspections by an architect to verify condition and assess what maintenance work is needed. Some grant-making organisations in the United States require grant recipients to donate a preservation easement as a condition of funding. An easement can also be used to raise conservation funding in other ways. For example, the Elfred's Alley Association in Philadelphia was set up to buy a number of row (terraced) houses built in the 18th century that had been left in a poor condition. The Association sold the properties once their market value had risen, each being subject to an endowment agreement, with the proceeds of the sale being invested in mutual funds so that grants and low-interest loans could be offered to the new owners to help them rehabilitate the properties. Owners can be offered grants of up to $5 000 and interest-free loans subject to the money being repaid within one year.

In the United States and Canada it is acknowledged that the use of an easement agreement has the effect of reducing the capital value of the property, generally by 5 to 20%, but in some instances the reduction in value has been assessed at 50% (as when a historic building is on a large parcel of land with development potential). For this reason, easement donations are accepted as being charitable contribution for tax purposes (if donated to a tax-exempt charitable organisation or public agency and subject to public access provisions), enabling any reasonable expenses related to the donation (such as legal and accounting fees, survey costs, recording and property appraisal fees) also to be tax-deductible. The tax savings can assist the owner in maintaining the property under the terms of an easement agreement.

Examples of easement holding organisations include the New Jersey Historic Preservation Trust in the United States and the Ontario Heritage Trust, Canada (see section 2.1.4).

2.6. Public authority bonds

In the United States, if a state or local authority issues its own debt in the form of bonds, the interest received on the bond is exempt from federal tax. This makes state bond issues competitive with company-issued bonds in terms of rates of return.

In a number of states (such as Maryland, New Jersey, New York and Pennsylvania) there is an authority to sell "bonds" to the public in order to raise funds for multi-year programmes to finance state capital projects, including the funding of heritage programmes. These have been justified by the better quality of life and the multiplying economic development created by such programmes. Economic studies to assess the benefits of heritage preservation have been essential in justifying the raising of money through bond financing, by identifying the increased return from increased tax revenues whether by income taxes from jobs created or property taxes or sales taxes according to materials purchased.

For example, legislation enacted by the State of New Jersey in 1987 created the Historic Preservation Bond Program, which authorised the sale of $100 million in state bonds to finance the acquisition and development of lands for recreation and conservation, and the restoration, rehabilitation and improvement of New Jersey's heritage resources. The legislation provided $22 million for a competitive grants programme and $3 million for a revolving loan fund to assist capital projects. It also authorised the New Jersey Historic Trust (a non-profit organisation) to administer the following programmes:

- The Historic Preservation Bond Program Revolving Loan Fund, providing loans of $25 000 to $450 000, with a repayment period of up to 20 years and interest rates below 4%. The trust was allowed to lend up to 90% of the project costs for non-profit entities and up to 40% for local and county governments;
- The Historic Preservation Bond Fund, providing grants from $25 000 to $1.25 million. All grant applicants were required to meet stringent criteria established in the Bond Act and the programme regulations, relating to eligibility requirements, research, architectural and

historical integrity, financial capability, public benefits and conform to Standards and Guidelines;

- An emergency grant and loan fund to provide seed funding for critically needed work (see also Chapter 4: Loans and credit facilities).

For grant assistance the Bond Act required 50:50 matching funds, and recipients were required to enter into an easement agreement to ensure maintenance of the property for a defined period of years, depending on the size of the grant. Between 1987 and 1997 the trust awarded between $50 and $55 million in matching grants to 108 projects.

2.7. Lotteries

A number of countries use the proceeds from public lotteries to support heritage projects. Lotteries can provide a useful source of finance, for example in Italy (for restoration of important monuments). In Germany, one third of the income from the Glucks-Spirale television lottery is given to the Deutsche Stiftung Denkmalschutz foundation (see section 2.2.5), raising €15 million or more per year for built heritage. In the Netherlands, the BankGiro Lottery (BankGiroLoterij) donates over €50 million per year to charities. Hendrick de Keyser (see section 2.2.3) is one of the institutions that benefits from the lottery. The BankGiro Lottery has also run an annual competition to support the restoration of a chosen historic building since 2006. In the United Kingdom, the National Lottery has transformed funding for the heritage since it was set up in November 1994.

2.7.1. Example: The National Lottery: Heritage Lottery Fund, United Kingdom

The National Lottery was established in 1994. It raises money for a range of good causes that benefit communities across the United Kingdom. From every pound sterling spent on lottery tickets, 28% goes directly to good causes, split between:

- arts;
- charities;
- health, education and the environment;
- heritage;
- sports.

Of money spent on lottery, 4.66% goes to heritage projects. This money is distributed by the Heritage Lottery Fund, which makes grants for projects concerning heritage anywhere in the United Kingdom. It is the leading funder of the heritage in the United Kingdom and covers the entire spread of heritage – buildings, museums, natural heritage and the heritage of cultural traditions and language. It assists groups and organisations with projects that:

- encourage more people to be involved in and make decisions about their heritage;
- conserve and enhance the heritage;
- ensure that everyone can learn about, have access to and enjoy their heritage.

This includes, for example:

- building repairs and conservation work;
- repairing places of worship of all faiths;
- buying items, land or buildings that are important to the heritage;
- supporting heritage-led regeneration;
- restoring historic landscapes and urban parks;
- improving museums, galleries and archives and their collections;
- making it easier for people to gain access to their heritage;
- increasing learning about recording and conserving our heritage;
- widening participation among people of all ages and backgrounds – especially people from communities who have not been involved in the heritage before.

From 1994, when the Heritage Lottery Fund was established, to July 2007, it had awarded £3.97 billion to more than 26 000 projects across the United Kingdom. In the heritage environment about £1 billion has been awarded in 4 000 grants to restore thousands of historic buildings and monuments. Award-winning architectural, new-build projects have also been supported. £380 million has been awarded to restore 245 historic, public parks ranging from urban and country parks to public gardens, squares, promenades and historic cemeteries.

The Heritage Lottery Fund has contributed more than £2 billion to regeneration projects in the United Kingdom, with £147.5 million having been given to 468 projects through its Townscape Heritage Initiative (see section 3.3.3.ii) or in partnership with English Heritage. These grant awards have delivered urban regeneration by bringing derelict buildings back into use, providing business units, low cost housing, creating and sustaining jobs. This investment often acts as a catalyst for the regeneration of a wider area while preserving its special character.

The fund has also supported a local heritage scheme set up with the Countryside Agency (since 2006: Natural England) to enable people to look after and learn about their local landscape, landmarks, tradition and culture, with £13 million being distributed to over 900 projects. Over 150 community groups have received funding to create community archives of maps, photographs, websites, videos and oral history recordings.

The decision to establish the Heritage Lottery Fund was as a result of the shortfall in public funding of heritage and also of the recognition that heritage matters to everyone in society. The Heritage Lottery Fund is committed to preserving this heritage for future generations to discover and enjoy, opening it up for the benefit of new audiences. It has a uniquely broad approach – which allows it to support many different causes that reflect the variety of heritage that is important to all kinds of people. It prioritises areas for funding across each of the United Kingdom's principalities and the English regions, ensuring a fair distribution of grants across the United Kingdom and throughout its communities.

2.8. Concession agreements

The particular difficulties in raising finance experienced by countries in eastern Europe have led to the use of concession agreements. Such agreements are relevant for heritage property in public ownership. In effect, a concession is a "right to use" for a monetary payment – a contract between the state (or local government) and the occupier or user of public property (including heritage assets). It creates obligations on the concession holder, which could include a requirement to perform conservation or restoration activities on a monument. For example, in relation to the use of a historic building in a medieval town a concession could allow the occupation of the building for tourism or other business purposes in return for a fee, with the payment being used to assist the conservation/restoration of the buildings.

This approach to raising finance has been considered in the former Yugoslav Republic of Macedonia, Bulgaria and other eastern European countries where the process of restitution of property to private owners remains incomplete. It offers a means to open up heritage to the private sector. In the absence of adequate financial support, the concept of "concessions" would seem to be a plausible approach to using the heritage with appropriate safeguards – which could be specified in contractual terms, though the normal procedures of control that should apply to monuments may be sufficient.

However, there is the danger that the concession approach is used to retain heritage property in public ownership for fear that the private sector cannot or will not manage it properly. It is therefore important that sufficient information and technical guidance is provided to assist private owners and private initiatives in preserving the cultural heritage. Moreover, whereas countries like France also use the concession approach for heritage property in public ownership, there are other methods of providing finance to private owners. The concession approach should not be a way of replacing financial support mechanisms.

2.9. Monument annuities

Another method of raising finance for heritage that is being considered by some eastern European countries is commercial exploitation of the heritage. This includes charging for the use of the image of cultural property or a "monument rent" for certain types of business activity carried out in heritage property or within a "cultural historic entirety" (this might cover hotels and restaurants, taxi services, banks and wholesale dealing in machines, equipment and accessories). Private individuals and legal entities that pay income or corporate tax in this situation would be liable to pay a rent at a defined percentage on income and depending on the location of the premises. This money would be directed to a "competent administration body" and the local government.

For example, measures for the commercial exploitation of the heritage as a means of revenue-raising through a monument annuity can be found in the Croatian Law on the Protection and Preservation of Cultural Goods. Under this law, the annuity is collected by two means.

Firstly, the monument annuity is collected by charging for direct consumption of a monument or monument site. Under Article 114 of the Croatian Law on the Protection and Preservation of Cultural Goods (1999, amended 2003), legal entities and individuals who are required to pay taxes on income or profits that use an "immovable cultural good" for economic benefit or perform commercial activity "in the region of a cultural-historical site" must pay a monument annuity. The basis of the annuity is the usable area of the business space and the amount charged ranges from 3 to 10 Croatian Kuna (HRK) per square metre of useable space (as decided by each municipality). Those individuals or legal entities that are required to pay the annuity must deliver information concerning the useable area of business space to the relevant municipal authority by 31 March of the year in which the monument annuity is established. Beneficiaries of concessions (see section 2.8) granted under the law are exempt from paying the annuity.

Secondly, a monument annuity can be collected through indirect monument consumption. The first legal provision for this form of monument annuity in Croatia was through the 1986 Law on the Restoration of Endangered Architectural Heritage in Dubrovnik. Under Article 51 of this special law for Dubrovnik, the use of the coat of arms or symbol of Dubrovnik or a recognised part of the monument site (or objects within it) on photographs, stickers, badges, souvenirs or other similar products was subject to a 10% surcharge on the retail price of the product, which the retailer was required to pay into a resource fund to maintain the Dubrovnik monument site. The implementation of this provision generated considerable funds for the historic city. As a result of this beneficial experience, new provisions were established by the Law on the Protection and Preservation of Cultural Goods to extend this procedure throughout Croatia as a method of raising income to finance work on protected heritage.

Article 112 of the law extended the 10% surcharge to the use of the image of any "recognised cultural good" (meaning monuments and the like) or part of it in "photographs, stickers, badges, souvenirs, publications and other written material, apparel items or other items". Furthermore Article 113 provided that legal entities and individuals that use a "recognisable cultural good" (or part of it) for promotional activities (in films, commercials, billboards, photographs or other items) are required to pay HRK1 000 for their use – the exchange rate being about HRK7.25 to €1 in 2008. An amendment to the 1999 law, created through the 2003 Law on Changes and Additions to the Law on the Protection and Preservation of Cultural Goods, introduced a new Article 114a, which required that particular named economic service activities (for example, taxi services, activities in travel and tour agencies, wholesale trades, hotels, restaurants and commercial banks – among 27 named activities) must pay into the national budget 0.05% of their realised annual income from the previous year as a monument annuity.

The money derived from these different types of monument annuity goes either to the state to be distributed by the Ministry of Culture (40%) or to the city or municipal authorities where it is collected (60%); see Figure 4. Revenues collected in this way can only be used for the protection and preservation of cultural heritage. However, though it is the responsibility of the owner of a protected heritage asset to ensure that it is maintained for future generations, these revenues can benefit owners who pay the annuity through the provision of financial assistance. Such assistance can be made available to cover the difference between the cost of fully implementing measures for the preservation of the asset, as prescribed by the conservation department of the Ministry of Culture, and the regular maintenance expenses.

The Croatian law presents a fairly balanced approach (balancing incentives against coercive measures). It allows aid to compensate for the additional restrictions that result from owning protected as opposed to ordinary property. At the same time the basis of the provisions is that, if an owner is not able to meet the obligations required by the law, their responsibility still remains, which may result in the owner being required to sell or relinquish the property. In theory this is justifiable, but any such procedures should be reasonable.

Monument Annuity: Dubrovnik, Croatia

In 2004 the Ministry of Culture of Croatia asked all city and municipal authorities to deliver a decision on the level of monument annuities and other estimated resources that the administrations were planning to collect. As at 23 September 2004 the total area for the urban site of Dubrovnik was 17 680 sq. m and the monument annuity was HRK2 102 122 (about €284 000).

In 2006 Dubrovnik had the fourth highest collected resources of all municipalities in Croatia from monument annuities per square metre, at €703 000, collected via Article 114 of the law. In 2006 Dubrovnik had the fifth highest collected resources from monument annuities at the rate 0.05% of income, at €176 000, collected via Article 114a of the law.

The total amount raised from monument annuities in all cities and municipalities in Croatia in 2006 was HRK163 100 000 (about €22 100 000).

Figure 4 – Houses in the Stradun, Dubrovnik, built after the 1667 earthquake.

These late 17th-century buildings are uniform in height and in the configuration of arched doorways and display windows at street level, and are purpose-built to accommodate shops. The monument annuity is based on the useable area of business space (direct monument consumption), but the souvenirs and other goods sold in the shops may be subject to a further surcharge (indirect monument consumption).

2.10. Transfer of development rights

This is a system of transferring development rights from one property to another, by which a property owner may sell or transfer a right to develop land on which a "historic landmark" (heritage building) stands. It originated in the USA and has also been used in Canada, Israel, Hong Kong and elsewhere. Such rights are associated with land-use planning systems that use zoning to define types of permissible land use – so a development or construction proposal that meets the requirements of permitted uses for that particular zone should be granted consent. This type of planning system is common in North America (USA and Canada).

By selling the development rights to a receiving site, the owner receives funding which is then committed to maintain and preserve the protected building. Although the situation is vastly different to that of eastern European countries in transition, the concept nevertheless has merit in raising finance for owners of heritage property to assist in conservation/rehabilitation.

The transfer of development rights derives from a planning technique known as "zoning bonus" – which, in this context, is a permit for increased density, granted as a trade-off for the inclusion of special amenities, such as preserving historic buildings within a development. It is a form of "enabling development" whereby an investor or developer uses the additional land associated with a historic building (for new construction) and gains consent for the development by agreeing to undertake enabling works to a historic building (see section 2.11). In theory the amount of the bonus should equal or slightly exceed in value the cost that the developer will incur in providing the amenity. This trade-off is advantageous to the public and the developer, as long as strict planning and design guidelines are adhered to.

The traditional concept of property rights in countries that use zoning assumes that zoning controls allocated to any given site will be used solely on that site, or will not be used at all. An innovation in zoning in North America is the reformulation of property rights to sever development rights from their host site for transfer to another zoned site. For example, in some states in the USA and some provinces in Canada a property owner may transfer or sell the right to develop land upon which an historic building lies to a parcel of land elsewhere in a town or city (see Figure 15). By selling foregone development rights to a receiving site, the property owner receives funding which can be partially used to finance the preservation of the historic building (and in fact there must be some form of legal commitment to maintain the building in the long term). There may also be an intermediate stage between severing and transferring, in which the development rights are placed in a development bank, created for the purpose of buying and selling these development rights, for eventual transfer. In effect, this system sets up a market for zoned development rights that can be transferred from one property to another. The transfer of development rights is particularly beneficial to places of worship (churches or buildings for worship of other faiths) and other non-profit property owners who are tax-exempt and cannot take advantage of tax incentives where they apply (such as the historic rehabilitation tax credit operated in the USA).

The transfer system necessitates planning controls to ensure that the aggregate density of the entire transfer district (where the right to develop is transferred) is not increased by the creation of the transfer regime and to avoid the undue concentration of development rights on any single transferee site within the district. Moreover, the legal validity of any new zoning restriction on a receiving site, to promote a specific public purpose such as the preservation of buildings in the public interest, would have to be addressed by the judicial system.

The ability to transfer development rights for the purpose of safeguarding a historic building works on the basis of a preservation restriction. Typical preservation restrictions detail the obligations placed on the owner for the long-term preservation of a historic building – usually tailored to meet the needs of the individual building. These can include restrictions on use of the building; the prohibition of material alterations or demolition; limitations on signs and on the subdivision of the land and/or addition of buildings to the site; conservation/restoration requirements, including agreed periods for the completion of works; obligations on the owner to keep a property in good repair (such as through a predetermined maintenance plan); and other procedures to cover such matters as remedial action for the breach of restrictions, the requirement to allow periodic inspections of the premises to ensure that the restrictions are being honoured and miscellaneous provisions, such as for public access to the building.

In practice these types of restriction may be legally determined as being perpetual or limited to a number of years (usually by a form of restrictive covenant, recorded through land registration to give notice to future purchasers and mortgagors). Moreover, it is normal for such preservation restrictions to be safeguarded by enforcement rights by public agencies or specific preservation associations (including injunctions to prevent damaging works or legal remedies to ensure that funds are committed for maintenance work).

This system for transfer of development rights may not sit easily in the context of European planning systems. However, it merits consideration as a means to resolve the dilemma of how to maintain historic buildings in places where development pressures may occur, a way of resolving the conflict between development pressures and preservation goals. Moreover, through the negotiation of legal agreements (or specific legislative tools) it may be a means to provide finance for historic buildings to ensure their long-term preservation, conservation, restoration or rehabilitation.

The only European country to have developed a system of transfer of development rights is Cyprus, which also uses a system of site-specific land-use zones (identified through local plans). Heritage protection forms a major component of the planning legislation through the Town and Country Planning Act 1972 (put into operation from 1990) and later amendments. Built heritage in Cyprus has been under threat from many causes (including the post-independence boom of the 1960s, the Turkish invasion of 1974 and more recently tourism development). To encourage restoration and revitalisation of listed buildings, a package of incentives was introduced through legislation in 1992, including grant aid towards restoration costs (up to 40% of approved costs for urban listed buildings and 50% for listed buildings in rural settlements and the countryside, which do not benefit from certain transfer of development right provisions), tax incentives (available once listed properties have been restored, to encourage maintenance) and the provision of low-interest loans. The provision for transfer of development rights is regarded as the most innovative measure and relates to plot ratio (applicable development density/building coefficient as defined in local plans) of a site.

The procedure for transfer of development rights in Cyprus is that any owner of a listed building is entitled to transfer the development rights attached to it (the donor building) to another building (the receiver building) in a specified commercial or tourist area anywhere on the island provided that legal requirements are met. In fact, the owner of a listed building can either transfer or sell square metres of permitted building area to another property through two separate procedures: residual building coefficient or donated building coefficient.

The transfer of what is known as the residual building coefficient (transfer of that part of the plot in square metres that the owner is normally allowed to build on, according to the Local Plan for the area in which the historic property is located, but cannot in fact do so because of other restrictions imposed by the fact that the property is listed under law). In this case, owners are permitted to transfer or sell the residual area of their listed property to any other area that has been established as a "user of coefficient". However, only buildings in urban areas may benefit from this incentive, because the land value in rural areas is much lower than in urban areas – so this measure would not be of practical value (properties in rural areas that do not benefit from this incentive can obtain a higher level of grant aid for restoration costs).

There is also another transfer incentive, available to owners of listed buildings anywhere in Cyprus (both urban and rural areas). This incentive is the donated building coefficient (or the "provided plot ratio"). This allows the owner of a listed building to transfer a certain number of square metres that the government allocates to each listed property so the owner may then transfer or sell these extra square metres to effectively increase the amount of grant aid that can normally be obtained for restoration work. This procedure may only take place before or during the progress of building works.

An application for a transfer of development rights has to be submitted to the Lands Office of the district where the property is situated in Cyprus and must include: a permit for transfer of the plot ratio (obtained from the Town Planning and Housing Department); certificates of registration of the properties; a statement referring to the manner in which the plot ratio is to be transferred and, in the case of sale, the consideration (price) for such sale; a certificate from the Town Planning and Housing Department on the payment of an amount equivalent to 10% of the value of the transferred/additional plot ratio determined by the Department of Lands and Surveys; and, where the property on which the listed building stands is encumbered (for example by a mortgage), the written consent of the person in whose favour the encumbrance operates. Once payment of prescribed fees has been made, the transfer of the plot ratio is registered by an entry in the Land Register and in the certificates of registration of the buildings concerned.

The development of a master plan for the largest town in Cyprus, Limassol, which aims to safeguard the preservation of architecturally significant buildings and historic districts, has envisaged a number of economic incentives for owners of historic buildings, including the transfer of development rights and specific tax incentives for restoration works. Because old buildings are generally regarded as inefficient and now often unusable, and are not developed to the maximum allowable limits by the zoning provisions in the planning law, they may become redundant. Therefore, the master plan envisages that owners of such "landmark" buildings should be permitted to sell the development rights of the plot to developers in areas that have been proposed to receive such rights:

- Within certain older areas of the city (to be designated as historic districts), properties that are recognised either as worthy historic buildings or as contributing to the historic character of the district should be granted the right to sell their development rights to districts designated as "recipient" areas;
- The waterfront zone between the Old and New Harbours, which has traditionally accommodated industrial uses, should be designated as an "area recipient" of development rights (with the possibility of developing mixed commercial and residential uses). This will enable developers within this district to increase the area of their maximum permissible building through the purchase of development rights from properties within historic districts.

The use of transfer of development rights as an enabling mechanism for conserving, restoring and rehabilitating architectural heritage in European countries is a relatively new phenomenon. However, the recent use of this type of mechanism in Cyprus could provide an exemplar, particularly to countries in transition.

2.11. Enabling development

"Enabling development" enables a heritage asset to survive by rescuing it from decay, bringing it back into beneficial use, securing its long-term future by some form of endowment, enhancing the asset or its setting by reversing past development, or making it more accessible to the public.

The concept of enabling development has been scrutinised in the United Kingdom. It relates to new construction activity that would normally be regarded as being contrary to approved planning policies, but which is occasionally permitted because it brings public benefits greater than the harm that would be caused by the development. So, in the context of historic buildings, if a developer offers to provide a community benefit by conserving a heritage asset in return for the grant of planning permission to develop that would not normally be given, this would outweigh harm created to other interests by such development. It can be regarded as a form of public subsidy: the public benefit created by contravening normal policy brings added value.

An example of enabling development would be the development of new housing in the grounds of a large protected country house that is not occupied and is in a poor state of repair, where the new houses provide sufficient funding for the repair and sympathetic rehabilitation of the building by conversion into apartments to ensure its long-term future.

This form of development is not normally permitted unless certain criteria are met:

- the enabling development should not materially detract from relative architectural, historic or other interest in the heritage asset, nor should it materially harm its setting;
- the proposal should not result in the detrimental fragmentation of the heritage asset;
- the enabling development should secure the long-term future of the heritage asset and, where a new use is necessary for this purpose, this must be sympathetic to the interest or qualities of the asset;
- the issue of enabling development should arise from the inherent needs of the heritage asset rather than the circumstances or profit motives of the landowner or the price given by the developer for the land;
- financial help (through subsidies or other sources) is not otherwise available for securing the heritage asset;
- the enabling development should be the minimum necessary to secure the future of the heritage asset and its form should minimise any disadvantages to it;
- the value of the benefit gained (in the survival or enhancement of the heritage asset) outweighs the long-term cost to the wider community of the enabling development.

If these criteria are met, this provides the basis for granting permission for the enabling development. This type of approach requires careful judgements in the balancing of benefits and disadvantages, ensuring at the outset that all aspects are considered. To ensure that heritage objectives are fully secured, the approach in the United Kingdom often uses a form of legally enforceable agreement (termed a "planning obligation") to ensure that the commercial element of the development cannot be carried out without the heritage benefits of the scheme being realised. Such agreements run with the land, so that any future owners are bound by the agreement. They are normally used to restrict the development or use of the land in a specified way, requiring certain action, payments to be made (such as for carrying out repairs to a historic building) and monitoring carried out during and after the works, and they are aimed at protecting the significance of the heritage asset in the long run. The financial element of the agreement should determine how the heritage asset is funded in the long term (in addition to the cost of repair or rehabilitation); this could be through a capital endowment (similar to an easement donation), through rental income from part of the enabling development or through other obligations to cover maintenance costs.

These types of agreement are usually necessary for this type of procedure to secure the defined objects. However, though enabling development may be a means to secure financial resources for heritage assets, it is a tool that is strictly controlled and rarely brought into play. There are dangers in relying on developers to provide finance because any developer can encounter financial problems, and practice has shown that conservation work deferred until the completion may not be realised. Therefore, enabling development requires careful monitoring both during and after the works.

Building Preservation Trusts (BPTs) in the United Kingdom, as property developers with charitable objectives, can have a role in enabling development schemes. This can be by repairing and managing a historic building funded by enabling development undertaken by a commercial developer or by the BPT buying and repairing a protected building and then selling it on to a developer for fitting out (perhaps for conversion to a new use) and marketing the property for sale. The bringing together of charitable (non-profit) or public agencies and private sector operators can result in a sharing of risks (the risks associated with the heritage asset and risks associated with the development) to ensure a more satisfactory outcome.

2.12. International and pan-European organisations

2.12.1. World Monuments Fund

The World Monument Fund (WMF) – founded in 1965 as an international non-profit organisation based in New York, London and Paris, with a European regional centre in Paris – is open to requests for assistance from interested parties around the world, including individuals, organisations and government bodies, in the conservation of cultural heritage sites. It receives nominations to join the World Monuments Watch (WMW) list of 100 Most Endangered Sites and applications for financial support for field conservation projects. The WMF is dedicated to protecting endangered significant architectural heritage sites throughout the world through advocacy, financial support, technical assistance and educational activities.

The biennial listing of the 100 Most Endangered Sites, which began in 1995, highlights the plight of threatened cultural heritage sites by raising their profile and attracting financial and technical resources. It aims to target specific sites at risk by devising financial and technical solutions. Sites on the Watch list are nominated by government agencies, non-governmental organisations, conservation professionals or concerned individuals through a formal review process. About 400 sites have been selected for assistance.

To be considered for inclusion on the WMW list, sites must meet three criteria:

- significance, in terms of its intrinsic artistic, architectural, historic, or social value;
- urgency, in terms of the need for immediate attention;
- viability, in terms of the possibility of finding a solution to save the site through advocacy or financial and/or technical assistance.

In providing financial assistance the WMF may commit restricted funds that it administers on behalf of specific donors or through challenge funds that result from fundraising efforts managed by WMF and its affiliates:

- restricted funding is available for projects that meet the criteria of one of WMF's restricted funding programmes;
- challenge funding is selectively awarded by WMF to projects compatible with its mission in order to attract local counterpart funding from private or public sector sources. Challenge funding is offered by invitation only.

Financial assistance from WMF supports conservation projects and initiatives in all stages of development, including preliminary assessment, planning studies, pilot projects, project implementation and training activities related to the conservation of a specific site. The

WMF also administers several funding programmes provided by external sponors.

- *American Express Grants*

The American Express Company was a founding sponsor of the World Monuments Watch programme. It has offered grants ranging from $10 000 to $100 000 to selected sites on the WMW list (publicly and privately owned) on a competitive basis and has partnered the WMF in a global initiative on sustainable tourism. In 2006 American Express launched a five-year programme with the WMF, Partners in Preservation, to safeguard significant architectural and cultural sites.

- *Kress Foundation European Preservation Program*

The WMF administers the Kress Foundation European Preservation Program for the Samuel H. Kress Foundation. This provides grants to non-profit organisations, cultural and academic institutions, government agencies and local communities for architectural conservation projects ranging in size from $25 000 to $100 000.

- *Jewish Heritage Program*

This programme was launched in 1988 with the support of the Ronald S. Lauder Foundation. The Jewish Heritage Program has addressed urgent conservation needs of historic synagogues at risk of losing their architectural integrity. It has awarded grants to more than 45 sites in over 20 countries.

- *Robert W. Wilson Challenge to Conserve Our Heritage*

The Robert W. Wilson Challenge to Conserve Our Heritage has provided matching funds for the conservation of sites on the World Monuments Watch list of 100 Most Endangered Sites. Finance is provided for field conservation work at sites of exceptionally high architectural significance, and for projects that foster partnerships with private and public institutions addressing architectural conservation needs.

2.12.2. Getty Foundation

The programmes of the J. Paul Getty Trust, through the Getty Foundation, support institutions and individuals throughout the world, funding a range of projects that promote understanding and conservation of the visual arts. There are two types of grant for architectural conservation, directed at organisations working to preserve buildings or sites that are nationally recognised as being of outstanding architectural, historical and cultural significance:

i. Planning grants

Planning grants assist in the drafting of an overall architectural conservation plan (support can also be given on a selective basis for the drafting of archaeological site management plans). The work must be for conservation planning rather than for reinstatement or rehabilitation.

Applications are considered for support of up to $75 000 for the research, documentation and analysis necessary to develop a comprehensive conservation plan covering the condition of the historic structure and fabric of a building, detailed conservation recommendations, plans for future use, and maintenance and conservation issues related to a building's setting. Projects can also cover temporary emergency conservation measures designed to stabilise a building while a conservation plan is being prepared. Planning grants often provide training opportunities for students or professionals in architectural conservation.

ii. Implementation grants

Implementation grants assist in the actual conservation of a building's historic structure and fabric. As with planning grants, architectural reinstatement and rehabilitation for commercial use are not normally eligible for assistance.

Applications are considered for support of up to $250 000 for the actual conservation of the historic structure and fabric of a building or site. These grants are intended to serve as models of conservation practice and are therefore highly selective. Grant awards usually require on-site training opportunities for students or professionals in architectural conservation or related disciplines.

To be eligible for either grant, the applicant must be a non-profit or charitable organisation and the building must be owned by a non-profit, charitable or otherwise tax-exempt body committed to its long-term preservation. The building must also be accessible to the public or otherwise used for the benefit of the community (see further: section 3.2).

2.12.3. Europa Nostra

Europa Nostra, a pan-European federation of more than 200 non-governmental heritage organisations, seeks to encourage the protection of architectural and landscape heritage. The federation is supported by the fees and donations of its collective and individual members, public bodies (including the European Commission Culture Programme), private foundations (such as the World Monuments Fund), corporate members and business sponsors, including European banking and real estate companies. The Europa Nostra Restoration Fund has made contributions of up to €20 000 towards the restoration of a privately owned endangered building or site with architectural or historical value, on condition that grant recipients source matching funds from other sponsors/donors. Europa Nostra has operated an award scheme recognising outstanding restoration of historic buildings or their surroundings, the restitution of land and the design of modern buildings that fit well into the sensitive environment of historic cities. Increasingly, Europa Nostra acts as a springboard to other European funding initiatives (such as those of the European Union) rather than offering its own assistance.

2.12.4. European Union

The European Parliament first considered the need for community action in the cultural field, including the need to protect cultural heritage, in 1974. The treaty establishing the European Community (1993) has provided the legal basis for activities concerning the preservation and enhancement of cultural heritage. Article 151 specifies that the Community must support and supplement action by member states in order to conserve and safeguard cultural heritage (in its broadest sense) of European significance.

The European Commission's 2006 study on *The Economy of Culture in Europe* highlighted two socio-economic spin-off effects of investing in heritage: the creation of local jobs and the development of corresponding skills; and the transforming of areas – in particular, cities – through the improvement of buildings "thereby increasing local attractiveness and generating significant returns on investments". Accordingly, the European Union supports cultural heritage, including architectural heritage, through a number of funding programmes:

i. Transnational funds

Preserving and enhancing Europe's cultural heritage was one of the key objectives of the cultural co-operation programme entitled Culture 2000, which lasted from 2000 to 2006. This supported projects for conserving European heritage of exceptional importance, such as the restoration of the frescoes in the Basilica of St Francis of Assisi in Italy. The programme also supported co-operation projects in the heritage field through the Europa Nostra awards granted to heritage restoration projects. This programme has been replaced by the EU's new Culture Programme (2007-13), which has a budget of €400 million for co-operation projects and exchange activities that aim to promote cultural diversity and preserve and enhance "shared cultural heritage" through the development of cross-border co-operation between cultural operators and institutions. This is aimed at projects lasting one to two years, where at least three countries are involved, and three-year co-operation projects with at least five countries for partners.

ii. Structural funds

In the period 2000-06, EU Structural Funds from the European Regional Development Fund (see Figure 1) were allocated to projects via regionally focused mechanisms (the three objectives) and via community initiatives, including the INTERREG III, URBAN, LEADER PLUS and EQUAL programmes.

For example, under Objective Two (for economically disadvantaged areas) of the regionally directed funding, a £35 million project to restore the Grade I listed town hall in the city of Birmingham, England was supported by £3 million of European funding.

An example of support from the INTEREG III programme is the INHERIT project, which ran from June 2005 to December 2007. This project aimed to increase the ability of towns and cities to regenerate physically, economically and socially by investing in architectural and other physical heritage with the key aim of understanding the processes that underpin successful heritage-led regeneration. The project involved partners from England, Italy, Northern Ireland, Poland, Spain and Sweden.

Examples of projects supported through the URBAN programme include:

- the restoration and conversion of the Tsalapata brick and tile factory in Greece, to create space for SMEs from the art and craft sector (total cost: €3 111 263; EU contribution: €2 333 477);
- the conversion of the historic Lasipalatsi building in Helsinki, Finland into a new centre of economic activity (total cost: €9 000 000; EU contribution: €2 700 000).

For the period 2007-13 the former URBAN and LEADER PLUS funds have been mainstreamed into main structural funds, which have three new objectives.

Objective One (Convergence Fund) supports those parts of the EU where the average GDP was less than 75% of the EU average. The priorities for funding include "investments in culture, including protection, promotion and preservation of cultural heritage; development of cultural infrastructure in support of socio-economic development, sustainable tourism and improved regional attractiveness; and aid to improve the supply of cultural services through new higher added-value services".

Objective Two (Regional Competitiveness and Employment Fund) replaces the objectives two and three programmes that existed in the previous funding period (2000-06). It is for other parts of the EU that are economically disadvantaged. The priorities for funding in this objective include the "protection and enhancement of the natural and cultural heritage in support of socio-economic development and the promotion of natural and cultural assets as potential for the development of sustainable tourism".

Objective Three (European Territorial Co-operation) replaces the INTEREG programme. It has two strands: cross-border co-operation and transnational co-operation. Under the first strand, a priority is the development of cross-border economic, social and environmental activities through joint strategies for sustainable territorial development, including by encouraging and improving the joint protection and management of natural and cultural resources, as well as the prevention of natural and technological risks. The second strand prioritises sustainable urban projects (among other matters), which include "preservation and promotion of the cultural heritage".

iii. Pre-accession aid

Pre-accession aid has been given to countries moving towards membership of the European Union. Recent schemes have included the PHARE programme, the Special Accession Programme for Agriculture and Rural Development (Sapard) and the Instrument for Structural Programmes for Pre-Accession (ISPA). These have been replaced by the Instrument for Pre-Accession Assistance (IPA), which offers rationalised assistance to countries aspiring to join the European Union for the period 2007-13 via a single framework. Assistance is provided on the basis of the European partnerships of the potential candidate countries (the former Yugoslav Republic of Macedonia, Croatia, Turkey) and the Accession partnerships of the candidate countries (Albania, Bosnia and Herzegovina, Montenegro, and Serbia including Kosovo as defined by the United Nations Security Council Resolution 1244).

Pre-accession aid can include assistance in relation to cultural heritage. For example, the IPAs for both Albania and Bosnia and Herzgovina (2007-09) include Component II: Cross Border Co-operation (CBC) in major areas of intervention. For both countries the CBC includes the "Adriatic Programme" which builds on the 2004-06 Italy-Adriatic Neighbourhood programme and specifies the protection and enhancement of the environment, culture and infrastructure of the cross-border territory. Also the IPA CBC programme between both Albania and Bosnia and Herzgovina and neighbouring countries in the western Balkans includes interventions in the sphere of economic and social development with particular reference to the preservation of cultural heritage.

2.12.5. Council of Europe Development Bank (CEB)

The CEB provides loans and loan guarantees for projects that are in conformity with the Convention for the Protection of Human Rights and Fundamental Freedoms and the European Social Charter. It operates along three sectoral lines of action: strengthening social integration, managing the environment and developing human capital. The protection and rehabilitation of the historic and cultural heritage forms one of three sectors in the "managing the environment" line of action and the CEB can finance projects that have been classified by UNESCO or member states under this theme.

During the 2007 financial year, loans to the value of €12 892 000 were granted by the CEB for projects concerning the protection and rehabilitation of historic and cultural heritage.

2.12.6. The World Bank

The World Bank operates through two principal mechanisms. First, the International Bank for Reconstruction and Development lends to developing countries (mainly financed by selling bonds on the global financial market, as well as by lending from its own capital resources). Secondly, the International Development Association provides interest-free loans (apart from a small service charge) and grant assistance to countries with limited or no access to global credit markets. Two types of loans can be granted through these two vehicles. Investment loans are made to countries to pay for goods, services and works to support economic and social development projects in a broad range of spheres. Development policy loans provide money that needs to be quickly disbursed to support policy and institutional reform. Grant aid can also be given to assist development projects by encouraging co-operation between organisations and local stakeholders in projects.

The World Bank has a long history of working in the sphere of cultural heritage, as is chronicled in its 2001 publication *Cultural Properties in Policy and Practice*. The World Bank's involvement with cultural heritage began with large-scale projects to support the restoration of historic buildings and landmark sites in the reconstruction of war-damaged places in post-war Europe. In the 1960s and 1970s the bank financed several infrastructure and tourism projects, including cultural property, and began to develop procedures to protect the environment, including cultural property. In 1989 the bank adopted an environmental assessment policy that referred to cultural property and the bank's work became more interdisciplinary, with greater consideration of cultural heritage issues. By the mid-1990s the bank had begun to explore the social implications of cultural heritage and in 1998 started the Cultural Heritage in Sustainable Development initiative (see Figures 5 and 6), later renamed Cultural Assets for Poverty Reduction. The World Bank's review of its role in cultural heritage recommended revising its policy to more systematically focus on safeguarding cultural properties and the way cultural resource activities relate to poverty reduction.

In recent years the World Bank has supported a Culture and Poverty initiative, aiming to reduce poverty by using culture as an asset, improving the effectiveness of investment projects by integrating cultural aspects into their design. This programme recognises culture as including architectural forms, historic sites and traditional technologies. It has been developed mainly because standard bank-financed projects do not generally respond to local cultural assets or practices. This programme has been supported by a grant from the Government of The Netherlands.

A World Bank-supported project in Georgia

The President of Georgia asked the World Bank and the Council of Europe to help the State Programme for Cultural Heritage Preservation. Following their positive response, a Cultural Heritage Initiative was launched and managed by new body, the Fund for the Preservation of Cultural Heritage of Georgia.

The project was the first specific cultural heritage project funded by the World Bank. On 18 February 1998 the Development Credit Agreement was signed by the Government of Georgia and the International Development Association in Washington DC, by which the World Bank allotted a credit of $4.5 million in the form of a Learning and Innovation Loan. The Government of Georgia contributed $480 000. The project collaborated with the Cultural Heritage Department of the Council of Europe via a Specific Action Plan. The basic aim was to rescue endangered heritage properties and test new approaches to managing the preservation and conservation of cultural heritage; therefore the project had two components: investment and technical assistance.

The investment component included an Emergency Repair Programme aimed at safeguarding endangered heritage properties all over Georgia and Four Pilot Projects (the Zemo Kala District of Old Tbilisi, Shatili, Sighnaghi and Uplistikhe), which envisaged restoration/rehabilitation of pilot sites and peparing for their sustainable development.

During 1998-99 a programme of restoration and rehabilitation work was carried out to listed residential buildings in the Zemo Kala District pilot project. The Fund for the Preservation of Georgia made available small grants for the restoration of facades, roof repairs, external painting, repairs to guttering and the restoration of balconies.

Figure 5 – Residential buildings in need of restoration and rehabilitation work in the Zemo Kala District of old Tbilisi, Georgia

2.12.7. The Aga Khan Trust for Culture

The Aga Khan Trust for Culture was created in 1988. Its financial resources are provided by His Highness the Aga Khan, as well as government bodies and private institutions. It supports single-site projects or regional projects throughout the Muslim world and aims to use culture to transform and improve the socio-economic conditions prevailing in many Muslim populations, especially communities that often have a rich cultural heritage but that live in poverty. It supports architectural heritage principally through two programmes.

Firstly, the Aga Khan Historic Cities Programme (AKHCP) was set up in 1992 to undertake the restoration and adaptive re-use of historic structures, the improvement of public spaces and the rehabilitation of urban areas to provide a catalyst to social, economic and cultural development in communities where Muslims have a significant presence. The programme also supports related socio-economic initiatives directed at upgrading local living conditions. The programme has an integrated approach and aims to show that strengthening cultural identity can go hand in hand with socio-economic progress (see Figure 6).

Secondly, the Aga Khan Award for Architecture (AKAA), established in 1977, recognises examples of architectural excellence, encompassing new buildings as well as conservation and restoration projects. It covers a wide range of issues, including contemporary design, social housing, community improvement and development, restoration and re-use of buildings, area conservation, landscaping and environmental issues. A triennial award of $500 000 is distributed among the projects selected by an independent jury.

The Aga Khan Trust for Culture also provides funding support to programmes of Tourism Promotion and Economic Development, and for the study of Islamic Architecture.

Where governments give subsidies from public budgets, these are provided by three principal methods: grants, loans and fiscal relief. These are considered in the next three chapters.

The Aga Khan Trust for Culture and other international funding organisations in the City of Mostar, Bosnia and Herzgovina

The Aga Khan Trust for Culture (AKTC) started work in Mostar in 1986 when the city was granted an Aga Khan Award for its "exemplary conservation, urban renewal and urban management efforts". After the 1992-95 war, in which much of the heritage was damaged, the AKTC joined forces with the World Monuments Fund in a partnership created under Robert W. Wilson programme with UNESCO, the World Bank, the local community and national and regional governments.

The original components of the project were the reconstruction of the old bridge (Stari Most), the adjacent towers of Tara and Halebija and associated buildings, the restoration of other damaged monuments and buildings in historic districts of the city, and local upgrading of infrastructure and open spaces to preserve the historic character of the area.

This programme of action lasted from 1999 to 2004, when the reconstructed Stari Most was opened. The AKTC and World Monument Fund then set up the Stari Grad (Old Town) Agency to oversee future rehabilitation and development in the historic city and to implement the Conservation and Development Plan for the Old Town, which was developed with the city authority in 2001.

Figure 6 – The reconstructed Stari Most (Old Bridge) and towers over the Neretva River in Mostar, Bosnia and Herzgovina.

This work was funded to aid a climate of reconciliation and to symbolise the restoration of peaceful co-existence among the three ethnic communities in Mostar. The work was carried out according to international standards and, where materials had to be replaced, stones were obtained from the original quarry used 500 years before.

3. Grant-aided subsidies

3.0. Introduction

Direct subsidies by awarding grants of money in line with public policy should take account of the nature of the operation. Preference may be given to maintenance, conservative repair or restoration of an individual architectural monument (building); which is chosen may depend on other factors, such as whether the monument is or is to be used exclusively for cultural purposes or for a socially useful purpose (such as social housing), or is capable of beneficial economic use (generating a profit or an income). This consideration may include a group of buildings of historic interest or in an area of cultural significance, whether protected or not. With particular reference to social housing, subsidy policy could be designed to encourage the conservation and rehabilitation of old buildings rather than the construction of new housing.

3.1. Grant-aid programmes

In the context of architectural heritage, grant subsidies take the form of payments by a donor government (or even a private philanthropic body) to a recipient public body (such as a local authority), non-profit organisation, private individual or private organisation, with the aim of stimulating activity by the recipient. Some grants require matching financial contributions from the grant recipient.

Essentially there are two types of grant programme. First are "formula" grants, which are not confined to specific projects. They are generally allocated by a central government or specific ministry to a local authority or other body responsible for heritage, for the purpose of distributing grant aid for specific projects. Secondly, "project" grants are meant to fund specific projects, usually concerning the conservation or restoration of protected buildings (but may sometimes include other buildings of cultural heritage interest). These grants are usually awarded through a competitive application process for a limited period. Once a project grant has been made, the donor organisation usually monitors and evaluates the result.

Project grants usually relate to conservative repair or restoration (reparation of architectural values), but not for maintenance or improvements (though under some schemes rehabilitation and improvement costs can be included, as in Germany). In some countries, a lack of financial support for maintenance after a repair grant has been given can lead to neglect, which may result in the inefficient use of finance through the need for further major grant-aided work in the future. However, maintenance work can be supported through standard conditions (as in England) or by specific subsidies for this type of work (for example, as in the Netherlands).

3.2. Administration and assessment criteria for grants

While grant programmes in operation are broadly similar, they vary greatly in specific characteristics like allocation criteria, administration, the degree of government regulation and the degree of control over their use exerted by the grantor.

The operation of a grant-aid programme is likely to require three principal phases. Firstly, the funding programme itself will require specific authorisation through legislation or regulation. Secondly, it will require a system for selecting appropriate recipients and allocating funds. Finally, it should have an assessment process to monitor how recipients have used the funds.

The identity of the administering agency is important since this agency typically has substantial discretion in determining how the grant programme operates. A crucial issue in the design of grant programmes is the determination of how grant funds are to be distributed. The administering agency for project grants, which are awarded on a competitive basis, defines the award criteria and ultimately chooses the recipients. With formula grants, a much greater degree of discretion in selecting recipients and determining the amount they receive is left in the hands of the administering agency.

The responsible agency must establish the regulations that it will use to operate the programme, detailing the following:

- administrative processes (application provisions, deadlines and appeal procedures);
- activities eligible for aid;
- duration and phasing of assistance;
- matching fund requirements and other obligations;

- weighting assigned to other criteria in making awards;
- monitoring and review process to determine performance; and
- any conditions.

3.2.1. Administrative process

Apart from specific regulations, explanatory documents should be issued to explain the process of applying for a grant. These should identify the priorities for assistance and the type of work that can qualify, explain how to make an application and how it will be assessed, identify how grants will be paid and how a project will be monitored, and explain the standard conditions that will apply.

3.2.2. Projects and activities eligible for assistance

The criteria for eligibility of buildings for assistance may be determined by various methods, such as by protection at a high level (where different levels of designation are considered by national legislation, bearing in mind that financial resources are finite). Different criteria can apply, such as regional or local importance or the need to undertake emergency/urgent repairs (based on an assessment of condition or threat, rather than national importance). Specific types of building can be given priority, such as religious or cultural buildings that are unlikely to have a beneficial economic use.

Normally heritage grants will dependent on the type of works proposed. They should primarily be used for urgent repairs or other work that needs to be undertaken within a relatively short time to prevent the loss of architectural features. Thus, alteration, improvement, demolition, reinstatement or reconstruction is not normally worthy of direct heritage subsidy. The priority should be conservative repair, though it may be appropriate for some grant schemes to give aid for the reinstatement of lost or destroyed elements where the integrity of the design has been kept and there is sufficient evidence to reliably undertake such work to regain the cultural significance of the building (speculative reinstatement or reconstruction does not merit support as it is against generally accepted notions of conservation philosophy according to international charters and conventions).

Although alterations and improvements such as new heating systems and insulation should not normally eligible for heritage grant subsidy, it may be appropriate for some grant schemes to provide financial assistance for redundant or under-used properties that are capable of being returned to use (the rehabilitation of a redundant protected building may be a means to ensure long-term preservation). It may be possible to pool subsidies from different sources, such as conservation grants for repairing historic structures and housing improvement grants for providing residential accommodation (see examples in Chapter 6).

Moreover, to sustain cultural heritage, some priority may need to be given to repair projects that will make a sustainable contribution to economic development – providing employment through tourism or the provision of business accommodation by rehabilitation of existing properties – or will provide significant social benefits such as housing, educational facilities or community resources. Properties that are incapable of being converted to a new use or of generating an income should only be considered as cases for financial assistance based on a formal assessment of need and financial priorities.

It may also be appropriate for grant aid to cover project development costs for a conservation project, including the formulation of conservation/management plans, feasibility studies and archaeological investigations and surveys. In some cases it may be necessary to undertake preliminary structural investigation, access and opening-up work to allow the scope of urgent works to be fully determined before a repair programme is initiated.

3.2.3. Duration and phasing of assistance

Most grant schemes are likely to pay the grant only when the work has been completed and approved as satisfactory. In some cases it may be necessary for a grant scheme to consider offering interim payments to meet cash-flow requirements (particularly for large or complex projects), but the normal approach should be to make such interim payments in arrears after the work has been carried out and an agreed point in the works programme has been reached.

3.2.4. Matching fund requirements and other obligations

Most grant programmes operate on the basis of offering a grant as a percentage of the total cost of approved works. This therefore can require the recipient to provide matched funding or a part of the costs (depending on the percentage offered by a particular grant scheme). In some countries, there are tax incentives to assist the owner in undertaking repair and conservation works (see Chapter 5), but where such incentives exist alongside grant subsidies the incentives normally apply only to the non-subsidised portion of the work.

Assessment of financial need for a grant subsidy can depend on a number of factors. Where properties are capable of producing an income or realising a profit, there may be restrictions on the award of financial assistance. It may be appropriate for the person who applies for financial assistance to show that there is a shortfall between antici-pated profits and the estimated cost of necessary works. For redun-dant or derelict properties it may be appropriate to assess the total cost of restoring or rehabilitating a property and its value after work has been completed, as a basis for assessing the need for financial assistance. There may also be some instances where subsidies can be provided without any assessment of financial need; this is likely to be so in the case of a property that is incapable of accommodating a beneficial financial use (such as a property to be used for cultural or religious purposes).

3.2.5. Weighting assigned to other criteria in making awards

Apart from building-type criteria for the eligibility of projects to be subsidised, the assessment of applications for grant aid can specify other requirements, such as:

- access – a requirement to allow public access to the property (for a limited and reasonable period);
- inclusion – where a project can provide social and education bene-fits for the local community;
- revitalisation – where a project can contribute to resolving problems of deprivation and to economic and social regeneration by bringing vacant property back into beneficial use, providing employment and housing, or where an exemplar project can act as a catalyst for further investment in the area;
- training and skills – where a project may provide training, and develop conservation and traditional building craft skills, particularly where such skills are in short supply;
- maintenance – requiring a commitment to maintain the property in the future;
- partnership – where the award of a grant may assist in levering funds from other sources (such as sponsorship) to preserve a property.

3.2.6. Monitoring and review process to determine performance

The regulations for grant assistance may need to specify how a grant-aided project should be monitored so the administrators of the scheme can check both progress and how well the funded works are meeting the aims set out in the application for assistance. This is particularly the case before any interim payment. In turn, this will suggest the need for regular reporting and supervision through site visits to confirm the quality and scope of the work carried out.

3.2.7. Conditions

Most grant regimes should be accompanied by standard conditions that may last for pre-determined periods and could depend on the amount of the award.

Conditions covering how the work is carried out will need to consider the contractual procedures for the type of enterprise that may undertake the work and, if supervised by the owner's professional representative, the type of professional who may undertake such work. In some countries this will necessitate specific qualifications for enterprises and professionals, though extensive experience in conservation work may also enable this criterion to be met.

Grant recipients should normally be required to submit financial records to a financial audit to show that funds are not being misspent. Grant-aided work may also require specific consent or approval under relevant heritage or planning legal provisions.

Conditions applying after the works have been carried out could relate to public access and the need for a maintenance plan (implying the need for annual reports on work carried out). The conditions could also require the repayment of a grant award (in full or part) if the recipient disposes of a property (by sale, exchange or lease) during the agreed period when conditions are still in force.

3.3. Examples of grant programmes utilised in different countries

Examples of grant-aid subsidy programmes can be illustrated from a number of countries.

3.3.1. Denmark

In Denmark, funding is directed at individual buildings; other funding can support built heritage through urban renewal programmes.

i. Individual buildings

Protected structures privately owned (by individuals or foundations) are entitled to receive a percentage of the costs of an approved scheme of works as ratified by the relevant government agency. Typically 20 to 50% of the cost of approved work required to preserve a building will be subsidised. The percentage depends on the nature of work and annual budget constraints – which can make it difficult for owners to establish the financial feasibility of projects. Complicated or expensive projects may receive a higher budget, theoretically up to 100%, though this is rare. Surveys are conducted of protected buildings at risk to help prioritise funding allocations, and grants may be given up to 100% of the cost of feasibility studies for protected structures to determine condition, necessary preservation works and the most efficient use for the building.

Grant recipients may borrow the money from a lending institution for the duration of the project, pending satisfactory completion and verification of the works by the government agency. If required, the government agency will agree to pay grant subsidy awards directly to the bank, instead of to the owner, on satisfactory completion of projects. The bank will be informed that the grant amount is dependent upon approval of work and provision of receipted bills. To ensure high standards of craftsmanship and materials, the work must be supervised by a conservation architect. Grant aid is only available for repair and conservation projects, and not for maintenance or the installation of modern facilities such as central heating or bathrooms. In addition to a grant award, support can be given in the form of materials from the government architectural salvage stocks. There is no public access requirement following receipt of grant aid.

Owners may combine state grants with private funding from foundations, investment funds or banks, for example. Foundations may provide top-up funding on consideration of the percentage of state grant aid that the applicant has already been offered for an approved scheme of works. The fact that a proposed scheme is entitled to state funding provides security that the lender's funds are being spent on a worthwhile project. For example, the Velux Window Company supports work on protected buildings through such a foundation.

ii. Urban areas

Urban renewal legislation in Denmark has resulted in public support for the renewal of buildings and urban areas that can benefit the architectural heritage, though it is not strictly focused on this (see Figure 7). A number of urban renewal instruments have been designed to encourage owners to make the decision to renew buildings. The state allocates an annual sum to support urban renewal initiatives administered by local authorities. The extent of public financial support for renewal projects is negotiated between local authorities and owners.

In some housing renewal schemes in older areas, care is taken to ensure that the area is not gentrified to such an extent as to displace existing communities. The financial support may be directed to the purchase and administration of a building by a social housing corporation within which tenants on social welfare benefits (unemployed or low income) are entitled to rental subsidies.

Some urban renewal schemes are based on grant aid, whereas others combine grants with loans or are purely loan-based (see further: section 4.1). Examples of grant-based schemes include:

- The Agreed Housing Improvement Programme (*Aftalt boligforbedring*), which has supported minor improvement or repair to privately rented and co-operative housing, based on negotiations and agreement between landlords and tenants.
- The Comprehensive Urban Renewal Programme (*Helhedsorienteret byfornyelse*), which has helped to co-ordinate regeneration of well-defined urban areas in need of renewal, other than renovation of buildings. In addition, 50% of the cost of preparing a master plan to identify problem areas is refunded by the state.

Some special schemes have been occasionally set up, for instance, to create work in areas of high unemployment, by providing special housing grants which support work to listed houses.

Urban renewal schemes assisting the heritage in Denmark

The municipality of Copenhagen initiated a comprehensive scheme of renewal for an enclave of housing dating from 1850, to act as a catalyst for citywide urban renewal projects.

The two-storey terraced dwellings were built to provide healthier housing after a cholera epidemic. By the 1980s the houses were in very poor condition and lacked modern sanitary facilities. Under threat of demolition, they were "listed" for their contribution to town planning. The renovation work, entirely paid from state funds at a cost of some DK300 million, was completed in 1996. Rehabilitation included the restoration of facades, the installation of replacement window frames and the provision of sanitary facilities at a cost of about DK1 million per dwelling.

Many of the buildings had been privately owned and occupied by their owners. They were expropriated by the municipality at a fair market value and then resold following restoration. The remainder of the buildings were in municipal ownership and let as social housing. The project took six years to complete due to logistical problems of re-housing the tenants while work was in progress. Former tenants wishing to return to the project had to pay an increased rent.

During this period the Minister of Housing gave the Copenhagen extra urban renewal funds spread over seven or eight years to renew similar housing projects.

Figure 7 – Housing complex in Copenhagen, Denmark,
saved from demolition through urban renewal funding

3.3.2. Belgium

Subsidy funding in Belgium is provided for classified buildings, groups of buildings and sites by the three regional administrations (with the exception of privately owned groups of buildings in the Brussels-Capital region). These grants, at varying percentages of the cost of works (ranging between 25 and 95%), are topped up for privately owned property by grants from municipal authorities and also by provincial authorities (except in the Brussels-Capital region). For example, restoration grants in the Walloon region are given in the following percentages: 60% (but 80 or 95% for special cases, such as buildings on Walloon's list of outstanding architectural heritage) by the region, from 1 to 15% by the province and from 1 to 10% by the municipality. Lower percentages are provided in the Brussels-Capital and Flemish regions.

Grants are offered by the Walloon region for certain eligible work, including the protection of monuments against damage caused by the elements or vandalism, urgent works such as weather proofing, stabilisation (sand consolidation), enhancement and major structural adaptation for new use. The eligible work also includes the cost of preliminary studies. Under the normal system of grant aid, up to 60% is offered to private owners by the region (higher in special cases).

In the Brussels-Capital region, the work covered by subsidies falls into two categories. Firstly, there is maintenance and repair work to ensure stability and protection against the elements, and this includes work for the preservation of structural components and the fitting of amenities (central heating or electricity, for instance). Secondly, eligible restoration work includes the restoration of component parts, the replacement of component parts where the state of dilapidation precludes maintenance, strictly documented replacement of valuable missing components whose absence is a major deficiency to be remedied, the removal of unsuitable components, additions and alterations, as well as the cost of preliminary studies. Under the normal system of grant aid, up to 25% is offered to private owners for restoration work by the region (with up to 40% for maintenance work for special cases).

In the Flemish region, eligible grant-aided work concerns maintenance and restoration. For restoration, grants up to 40% have been given to private owners (split between the region 25%, province

7.5% and municipality 7.5%), with up to 80% given for special cases – where, for example, the building is without an economic use (split 50%, 15%, 15% accordingly). These grant levels are generally subject to a ceiling figure on total cost. The regional authority ranks restoration grant applications in order of merit with regard to the physical condition of monuments, the number of years that monuments have been waiting for funding, the intrinsic value of the monument and potential use of traditional craftspeople. Monuments that have waited more than three years for a restoration grant are considered a special priority. The regional authority also favours phased restoration projects in order to avoid large-scale expenses. If it is likely that a monument must wait a number of years before receiving a restoration grant, the regional authority may arrange a maintenance grant to prevent further decay.

Since 1993 the take-up of maintenance grants has been encouraged on the basis that prevention is better than cure; maintenance is better than restoration as owners can do maintenance work in a faster and less complicated manner with financial support, and so they do. The level of maintenance grant varies between different provinces in the Flemish region. The maintenance grant can be applied for every year and the application procedure is simpler (taking about three months) than that for the restoration grant. As a result, owners of heritage monuments are encouraged to carry out regular maintenance rather than costly restoration.

The ministry recommends that prospective grant applicants use the Monumentenwacht (Monument Watch) service and its status report to guide them in forming a plan of works. This provides a platform for prioritising action because each element of a monument is categorised by its condition: good, reasonable, moderate or bad (see Figures 8 and 9). In some provinces in the Flemish region, membership of Monumentenwacht is an obligatory part of the grant application procedure. Monumentenwacht is based on a similar organisation in the Netherlands – see section 3.3.6.

Combination funding with project support from Monumentenwacht

Originally a rich merchant's dwelling built in the 15th century, Reyndersstraat 18 was converted to a monastery in 1902 and used for this purpose until 1974. It has now been restored following the recommendations of Monumentenwacht.

The owner joined the Monumentenwacht organisation and asked for grant aid based on yearly inspection reports of different parts of the building (as it was too large and complex to do as a whole). The programme of works included stabilising walls, restoring wall paintings and other works in the former monastery chapel, restoring traditional window frames (removing plastic frames inserted when the building was a monastery) and work to façade renders and to roofs.

The Flemish Region department responsible for heritage gave a maintenance grant of 40% up to a ceiling (with some further works being supported at 25%). The owner set up a company for the building, which enabled the non-grant-aided part of the cost to be deducted from business profits. During the work, part of the premises was let to a café/restaurant and part was used for concerts, with the rent from these being mainly ploughed back into the building to assist the programme of works.

Figure 8 – De Groote Witte Arend, Reyndersstraat 18, Antwerp

Front façade re-rendered through a reversible construction method and new window frames replacing UPVC frames.

Figure 9 – De Groote Witte Arend, Reyndersstraat 18, Antwerp

Courtyard café bringing in income to support the programme of works, including restoration of the wall frescoes dating back to 1480.

3.3.3. England

In England, grants for conservation work are administered for architectural heritage largely through English Heritage, an executive non-departmental public body sponsored by the central government's Department of Culture, Media and Sport, and the Heritage Lottery Fund (supported by the National Lottery, which was set up in 1994). Apart from specific heritage funding initiatives, other grant assistance has been provided for historic buildings largely through regeneration funding mechanisms (see example in section 6.2.4).

i. Historic buildings

English Heritage provides grant aid to owners of listed buildings in grade I or II* category (the highest categories, forming about 6% of the

400 000 protected buildings in England) as well as protected ancient and archaeological monuments and some designed historic landscapes. Exceptionally, grant assistance may be given to the remaining grade II listed buildings and other unlisted buildings of significant historic or architectural merit. Grant assistance is also given to local authorities to assist them in using statutory powers to force owners to carry out necessary urgent works to buildings considered to be at risk (such as through disrepair or vacancy), or to compulsorily acquire them, and for public-realm work for repairing and reinstating historic street works.

Grant aid from English Heritage for private owners of important listed buildings (grade I or II*) is prioritised on a national and regional basis with particular reference to whether a building is at risk from neglect or disrepair (usually by reference to a building being recorded on a Buildings at Risk register) and where alternative sources of funding are lacking. The need for financial assistance has to be demonstrated by applicants, and assistance is usually given for project development work (preparation of specialist reports as a basis for repair work) and for urgent repairs or other work that should be carried out within a two-year period to prevent loss or damage to important features, as well as associated professional fees. Assistance generally does not cover alterations and improvements, basic maintenance (such as decoration), demolition, reinstatement or reconstruction work. Exceptionally, where a building has kept its integrity in design, the reinstatement of lost or destroyed architectural elements may be grant-aided so long as there is sufficient evidence to ensure a correct form of restoration. Grant aid used to be given as a percentage of the total eligible cost of works but since 2005 it has been based on the priorities of perceived need and the demands of a limited budget with a restricted number of larger projects being considered (projects costing less than £10 000 not usually considered for grant aid).

An award may be subject to conditions in how the work is carried out (competitive tendering, copyright and other consents, and European Community procurement requirements) and after the work has been completed (public access, maintenance, repayment following sale of a property). The amount of public access is decided on a case-by-case basis with regard to the effect on the building and the size of grant provided. A costed Maintenance Plan may also be required, indicating work to be carried out, with an annual report on action taken. The sale or lease of the property may also result in the grant being clawed back if the conditions are still in force. Special grant schemes have also been provided for cathedrals, other places of worship (in association with the Heritage Lottery Fund) and war memorials, which cannot have a beneficial economic use.

The Heritage Lottery Fund also provides a programme of heritage grants for historic buildings (and other issues including nature conservation, museum and archive collections, spoken history records, cultural traditions, and objects and sites relating to the UK's industrial, transport and maritime history). The grant is offered to non-profit organisations (including local authorities, the National Trust and building preservation trusts) to assist the acquisition, maintenance and repair (including conversion of a historic building to provide a viable long-term use) of land and buildings of outstanding scenic, historic, aesthetic, architectural or scientific interest. The programme offers grants of £50 000 or more (there is no upper limit). An initial project planning grant has also been given (between £5 000 and £50 000 to help produce an access plan and conservation management plan, carry out research and employ a project officer to plan the project), but since 2008 this is no longer offered.

ii. Historic areas

Area-based funding mechanisms have focused on designated conservation areas since the early 1990s, centring on the idea of conservation-led regeneration.

Conservation Area Partnership Schemes (CAPS), in operation from 1994 to 2001, introduced the idea of conservation-led regeneration by tackling economic, social and physical urban problems in parallel through the formation of strategic partnerships (combining the aims and financial resources of organisations such as regional development agencies, specific regeneration budgets and European Union finance programmes). CAPS were managed by local authorities and funded jointly by English Heritage and local government. To be eligible for funding, the local authorities had to demonstrate a commitment to heritage conservation and make a financial contribution to the project. Through this scheme, varying percentages of grant aid were offered to owners of historic buildings according to an agreed scheme of finance, and local authorities gained access to finance to improve public space such as historic streetscapes (the public environment of a designated area).

Heritage Economic Regeneration Schemes (HERS) were introduced in 1999, essentially replacing the CAPS, and funding was provided in a number of bidding rounds until 2002 (though some schemes continued to run to 2006) specifically for historic areas with economic and social problems. Similar to CAPS, HERS were administered by local authorities that put forward bids annually for English Heritage funds to manage a scheme in their area. Bids for HERS had to be co-ordinated through an area-based strategy covering five key objectives:

- Rescuing buildings at risk and those vulnerable to deterioration;
- Investing in the regeneration of an area, including re-use of buildings that are important to economic prosperity and future local employment opportunities;
- Reinforcing, revitalising or renewing the economic base of an area;
- Encouraging the re-occupation of underused upper floors above high-street properties, (local businesses and shops), for residential or employment-generating activities, thereby helping to bring life back to declining town and village centres;
- Assisting with building repair costs, to help sustain the broader economic contribution made by local business to the local community, and to increase employment opportunities or residential accommodation to meet local needs.

The funding scheme allowed the preparation of bids for money from English Heritage which had to be matched by the local authority. The programme encouraged sourcing of additional funding through partnership with other public and private sources for regeneration purposes. HERS schemes could run for a maximum of three years and allowed local authorities to administer grants to third parties. Eligible expenditure included repair work relating to structure or external appearance of a building or the enhancement of conservation areas. Management costs could also be eligible in the scheme. Routine maintenance, alterations or conversion work were not eligible for grant aid. Applications for grant aid through a HERS could be made by private owners, small commercial owners and those responsible for environmental enhancement (see example in section 6.2.4).

In 2004 English Heritage published a document entitled *Funding for local authorities: partnership schemes in conservation areas*. This area-based funding programme builds on the HERS concept and is similarly for schemes of funding up to £100 000 per annum. The Partnership Scheme approach is slightly different, with a greater emphasis on sustainable development. The aim is "to secure a sustainable future for the historic environment" by ensuring that funding is directed to five key areas:

- Repairing historic buildings and bringing them back into use;
- Investing in the social and economic regeneration of England's urban and rural communities, including the creation of safe and sustainable communities;
- Ensuring work realised is sympathetic to the historic importance and character of an area;
- Completing works to an appropriate standard and ensuring that subsequent regular maintenance will be carried out;
- Ensuring that the work done is sustained by the local authority's policies and actions for the area.

The national priorities for Partnership Scheme grant funding include projects where significant elements of the historic environment are at risk and/or projects where there is a lack of alternative funding (and there may also regional priorities to consider). Eligible projects must be based within a designated conservation area and must be able to attract partnership funding from the local authority, and possibly other funding partners, and involve a range of work to a number of buildings, structures or spaces within a defined area. Projects must also target at least 60% of the partnership funding towards building repairs and require property owners to contribute financially towards grant-aided work to their property.

The Partnership Schemes can provide grants for the same type of work considered by HERS (major repairs to historic buildings, authentic reinstatement, public realm works) and can cover management and administration costs (for example, to support a project officer). A scheme cannot be used to finance demolition, conversion and alteration, modernisation, the provision of building services, or work eligible under other funding schemes.

An application for a Partnership Scheme first involves a preliminary application, including a map of the conservation area showing the extent of proposed scheme, photographs showing the scale of problems, a conservation area appraisal, a vacancy survey, a condition survey, a Buildings at Risk register, the indices of deprivation for the area and its employment rates. A detailed application must include a description of the special architectural and historic features of the conservation area, the problems faced by the area and the suggested programme of works, and an analysis of the conservation area in terms of its economic base, service and retail activity, business confidence, tourism potential, housing and social mix, identity and coherence, and opportunities for building on the area's strengths. The application must also explain why funding is needed, specify what planning policies have been adopted to support and sustain local economic activity, and indicate the aims of the scheme such as public benefits of access and interpretation, social inclusion, regeneration, training and skills, sustainability and partnership funding.

The approval of a scheme brings a further requirement to provide feedback on progress made towards an agreed delivery plan year by year. Without this, funding allocations cannot be confirmed for subsequent years of the scheme.

The Heritage Lottery Fund (HLF) launched the Townscape Heritage Initiative (THI) in 1998, and projects throughout the United Kingdom have been eligible for assistance. Similar to HERS and Partnership Schemes, THI schemes have been directed towards the problems of an historic area in parallel with economic regeneration, sustainability and raising the vitality and confidence of the community. The annual budget for THI will be £10 million for the period 2008 to 2013.

The eligibility of areas depends on an assessment of both heritage and economic needs. The partner organisations eligible to apply for a THI scheme include local authorities, regeneration companies, non-profit bodies and community groups. The partnership forms a common fund using funding from the HLF and other public or private sources. The HLF contribute to a common fund for each THI. Heritage Lottery funds directed to THI regeneration schemes support the repair of sensitive historic buildings and their environs rather than the area regeneration budget as a whole. HLF funding has typically ranged from 20 to 50% of costs (up to 75% in exceptional cases). THI funding has aided specific purposes:

- Repair of the structure and external envelope of historic buildings and structures. Maintenance costs are not covered and internal repairs are only eligible to ensure structural stability or allow public access. The HLF stipulate that grant levels to support eligible repair work should reflect the difference between the cost of repairs and the resulting financial value added to a property.

- Authentic reinstatement of architectural features to historic buildings and their settings, provided the fabric is in sound repair or will be repaired as part of the project. The HLF will not support conjectural restoration or other works to remove previous alterations of architectural or historic interest;
- Bringing vacant floor space in historic buildings back into economic use, including unused upper floors over shops. Support will normally be given to cover the difference between the cost of conversion (and repair) and the value when converted. (This continued a previous funding scheme called LOTS: Living over the Shop – see examples in sections 6.2.3 and 6.2.4);
- Removing visual degradation by filling gap sites in established frontages with buildings of appropriate use and demonstrating a high standard of contextual design, using natural materials indigenous to the area. Where economic conditions for the area indicate that appropriate quality can only be achieved via subsidy, the difference between the cost of developing such an infill site and its end value may be eligible for financial support;
- Repair and authentic reinstatement of elements lost from urban green spaces, historic surfaces and other "public realm" townscape features defining historic spaces. Conjectural restoration of lost features, replacement of street furniture and modern layouts will not be funded. The level of support is decided with reference to the cost difference between repair to normal standards and the conservation option.

Further financial support can be given for staffing costs and overheads to run a THI scheme (for example, project officers, consultants and marketing). In addition, the common fund of the THI can support complementary activities, such as the creation of a town trail, training initiatives to improve conservation skills, research of the area or other work related to the long-term management of the area. If an application for a THI scheme is initially accepted, then 75% of costs up to £25 000 for developing the project may be offered by the HLF.

Proposals for THI funding are judged on the historic merits of a scheme, the conservation and public benefits, the need for public-sector investment to solve major problems, technical quality, financial viability and organisational strength.

Generally, areas already supported by other schemes such as HERS or Partnership Schemes via English Heritage are given a low priority.

However, the funding for THIs is at a higher starting point. Applications for a THI grant contribution towards the common fund from the HLF were for schemes of £250 000 to £2 million, but since 2008 the minimum is £500 000.

The level of grant offered to individuals and organisations for different types of work through the common fund can vary – the advice is that each THI scheme should set grant-aid levels to achieve the desired effect and be based on the principle that public benefit should outweigh private gain. They usually do this by grants of a fixed percentage of the cost of specific work.

Both the English Heritage HERS/Partnership Schemes and THI schemes have been concentrated in designated historic areas (conservation areas) suffering from economic and social decline. Such areas are subject to preservation and enhancement plans in approved development plans. These programmes have been directed towards regeneration, using the built heritage as a factor in improvement of areas and communities. Such schemes have enabled the repair and rehabilitation of buildings for housing and commercial uses, as well as cultural purposes. Moreover, the funding has sometimes been used to provide social housing.

3.3.4. France

In France funding is given for historic monuments, protected areas and other ancient centres.

i. Historic monuments

Restoration and maintenance work on classified historic monuments may be eligible for state grant aid of 40 to 50% of the cost of approved conservation works. Grant aid towards approved works on monuments listed with the title of historic monument cannot exceed 40% of the cost. In practice, grant aid in either category can be up to 20% of total cost and is sometimes higher. Supplementary regional grant aid varies greatly from region to region. As a rule, communes do not grant financial assistance for historic monuments owned by private individuals (but may give assistance to historic monuments privately owned by institutions such as universities). Work on monuments owned by communes is funded 50% by the state (25% by the *département* and 25% by the municipality). The state may also pay 100% of the cost of research studies in connection with the preservation of historic monuments and their surroundings.

ii. Protected areas

There are three types of protected area:

- Conservation Areas (*secteurs sauvegardés*) of which there are about 100 designated;
- Architectural Urban and Landscape Heritage Protection Zones (ZPPAUPs) of which about 450 have been designated, with about a further 600 zones under consideration;
- Land-use plans can make special regulations to take account of the heritage features of parts of towns.

Funds have been provided for studies in connection with policy on enhancement for *secteurs sauvegardés* (the state supplying up to 100% of the cost, with increasing funding by communes in recent years) and ZZAUPs (where costs are divided equally between state and commune). Communes may initiate studies for other older areas to be protected and enhanced.

Regulations for these three types of protected area may provide for operations to assist restoration and rehabilitation. The state is now short of funds and rarely gives grant aid in this context, but many communes are able to provide grant aid assistance. In particular, communes sometimes provide grant-aid assistance of up to 20% of costs in relation to the rehabilitation of houses for sale or rent.

The rehabilitation of residential property in old parts of towns ("ancient centres"), whether protected or not, is also supported in "planned housing improvement operations" (Opérations Programmées d'Amélioration de l'Habitat or OPAH) – a scheme which, since it started in 1977, had by 2000 resulted in 3 000 such OPAHs and the rehabilitation of over 600 000 dwellings (mostly in old quarters and historic districts). An OPAH is a contract entered into for three years between the state, the National Housing Improvement Agency (Agence Nationale pour l'Amélioration de l'Habitat or ANAH) and a local authority or group of local authorities. ANAH is the main body for grant provision, whose role is to subsidise work undertaken by private landlords, but the OPAHs can also gain support from the state, the region and the municipality through other financing schemes (see Figures 10 and 11).

The OPAHs have a number of objectives: to provide healthy standards in living accommodation (to improve sanitation and resolve problems associated with lead paint), to improve heating and insulation, to assist co-owners of housing that are in financial difficulty, to undertake works of architectural repair and improvement (such as reinstatement of traditional roofs and windows) and to encourage lower rent levels (grant aid being given on the basis that an owner will agree to let apartments at a low rent level – a "renovation lease").

The renovation lease scheme set up by ANAH, in conjunction with the French ministry responsible for housing, provides a subsidy-funding vehicle for owner-landlords to finance works to substandard vacant housing while retaining ownership of their property. Renovation leases vary from 10 to 15 years. The renovation lease confers a right on the owner landlord to use the building in return for the payment of rent; that is, when the work is completed, the landlord manages the property as rented accommodation. The landlord must tender guarantees that rehabilitation works and subsequent management will be conducted in a sensitive manner. (See further examples of OPAH schemes in section 6.2.3).

It should also be noted that the rules governing ANAH allow the agency to offer one-off small grants and it can offer additional funding for buildings of architectural interest in *secteurs sauvegardés* and ZZAUPs, as well as OPAHs with a heritage component.

Tax relief and subsidies in the protected historic core in Troyes, France

The municipality of Troyes first defined the perimeter of a *secteur sauvegardé* covering 22 hectares on 21 September 1964, only two years after the Malraux Law ("Loi Malraux") was introduced (4 August 1962). It was subsequently extended in 1968 (to 29 hectares) and in 1975 (to 53 hectares). It was one of the first municipalities to request the formulation of a Plan de Sauvegarde et de Mis en Valeur (PMSV) which was subsequently approved and published 19 May 2003, establishing the rules of architectural restoration, urban planning and development for the area. The protected area was extended again when the plan was developed, now amounting to 180 hectares.

In parallel to the PSMV, a third OPAH initiative was launched principally to financially assist landlords with residential property in the protected area who wanted to rehabilitate their property. The primary objective of the OPAH, which commenced in 2004 lasting until 2009, is to solve the problem of vacant dwellings with unhealthy conditions and to rehabili-tate them. Approximately 700 residential units have been subject to the OPAH. A second objective of the OPAH is to enhance the built heritage of Troyes. (Two previous OPAHs had been operated between 1993 and 1996, and 1998 and 2002).

In 2002 the municipality decided to extend its protective measures by commencing studies for a ZZAUP, to cover areas of the industrial and textile heritage, which were subsequently approved in 2005.

Financial assistance is provided to landlords of tenanted residential property through the tax incentives offered by the *secteur sauvegardé* according to the requirements set out in the PSMV by which the cost of eligible works can be deducted from global income for tax purposes.

Figure 10 – Property awaiting rehabilitation within the perimeter of the Troyes secteur sauvegardé

The OPAH provides grant aid for two types of residential property owner: first, where the owner lets the property or the property is unoccupied. In this case ANAH provides grant aid for upgrading the accommodation at 20%, 35% or 50% depending on the type of tenant, with the highest rate applicable where the property is to be let to tenants on low income, and the municipality of Troyes provide grant aid of between 10% and 40% specifically relating to the restoration of façades or roofs visible from the public domain. Secondly, in the case of owner-occupied residential property, grant aid is provided by ANAH for upgrading works at 20% subject to a ceiling of €11 000 or 35%, subject to a ceiling of €13 000 for owners with a low income and by the municipality of Troyes (10% to 40% specifically relating to the restoration of façades or roofs visible from the public domain or accessible to the public) and complementary aid is given to retired owners.

Figure 11 – Rehabilitation of buildings in rue Emile Zola, Troyes with financial assistance provided by an OPAH

3.3.5. Germany

In Germany subsidised financial support is provided by various building funding programmes and specific heritage funding programmes.

i. Grant-aided building funding programmes

Monument owners in the designated building programme areas apply for funding via municipalities from three sources of government funding – federal, state and municipal. The municipalities provide 20% of the funding and the federal and state administration each provide 40%, although in practice many municipal authorities in eastern states have been unable to provide their entire funding obligation. Every municipality must define the percentage of restoration costs that will be provided from public funding, thereby setting the level that the owner will have to pay. On average, owners receive about 90% from public funds, provided they comply with an approved scheme of works.

A number of federal grant-aided building programmes have been initiated in Germany in the context of town renewal, with federal government involvement. The *Stadtbauforungsgesetz* programme in West Germany was resourced equally from the federal, state and municipal levels of government. After reunification (1991), a similar programme was initiated in the east, the Urban Architectural Heritage Protection in Eastern Germany (*Städtebaulicher Denkmalschutz*). This programme has been financed by the Federal Ministry of Transport, Building and Housing (Bundesministerium fur Verkehr, Bau und Wohnungswesen) providing funding to eastern states to aid the renewal of historic cities and towns by the maintenance, preservation and modernisation of individual buildings and groups, and the preservation and restructuring of streets and urban spaces of historic, artistic or urban importance.

ii. Grant-aided heritage funding programmes

A number of specific heritage funding programmes have been provided in Germany (which can be combined with the above building funding programmes):

- The *Stadtbauforungsgesetz* grant programme, which funds architectural heritage restoration projects, is administered by the state cultural heritage authorities (*Landesdenkmalamt*), either the Ministry of Culture or the Ministry of the Interior in each state. Owners in receipt of grant aid to finance restoration projects must comply with conditions such as restoration guidelines for individual buildings and streetscapes, and rent restrictions for agreed periods.
- The *Dach und Fach* (fabric maintenance) programme in the eastern states was initiated in 1996 by the Federal Government Commissioner for Cultural and Media Affairs (BKM) to fund the protection

of architectural monuments of local or regional historical and architectural importance in rural regions of the eastern states and the eastern part of the City of Berlin. The objective of this programme has been to provide emergency assistance to repair the external fabric of monuments at risk in order to prevent further deterioration pending renovation.

- The Conservation of Cultural Heritage Sites of National Importance programme, financed by the Federal Government Commissioner for Cultural and Media Affairs (BKM), provides financial assistance for the conservation of architectural monuments, archaeological sites and historic parks and gardens that demonstrate the nation's cultural, political, historical, architectural, scientific or urban planning achievements or have influenced the cultural and historic development of German cultural landscapes.

- The Historic Cities Support programme, funded by the Federal Ministry of Transport, Building and Housing (Bundesministerium für Verkehr, Bau und Wohnungswesen) to subsidise urban renewal and conservation initiatives in historic city centres.

3.3.6. Netherlands

A number of different grant-aid mechanisms have been offered in the Netherlands.

i. Restoration grants

The state budget for restoration subsidies is divided up between provincial and municipal authorities (depending on the number of monuments in a municipality area). Every year the municipalities must supply the state with a four-year future restoration programme, including details of proposed restorations. Budget allocations are administered by the Nationaal Restauratiefonds (National Restoration Fund), which is a private foundation. Municipalities are then given an allocation of funds (based on planned provincial and municipal restoration programmes and pre-defined quotas by building type: 50% for dwellings and farms, 30% for churches and 20% for castles, windmills and water-towers).

Grants range from 20 to 70% of certified restoration costs, depending on building type and the owner's tax liability. Taxpayers are entitled to a 20% grant, with additional income tax relief and/or a subsidised loan. Thus, a private heritage restoration project can be funded through

20% grant aid, 30% income tax relief and the remaining 50% through a low-interest loan at as little as 1% over a period of 30 years. Private individuals not in a position to claim income tax relief may be entitled to an increased grant of 50% of certified restoration costs. Tax-exempt bodies, foundations and parish churches are entitled to a 70% grant of certified restoration costs. When the building is publicly owned, a 60% grant of certified restoration costs may be given.

Grant recipients must wait up to five years for the 20% grant allocation. The National Restoration Fund offers an option whereby recipients may draw down the amount of the grant allocation in the form of a loan immediately and pay a very low rate of interest per annum.

ii. Maintenance grants

A state-funded maintenance grant of 50% of costs is available for non-income producing monuments such as churches, castles, fortifications, windmills and factory chimneys to protect structures against the effect of wind and water. Houses and farms are not entitled to this grant because maintenance expenses on these properties may be deducted from income tax.

A special note must be made about the Stichting Federatie Monumentenwacht Nederland (Monument Watch), which was set up in 1973 to encourage owners of historic buildings to undertake regular maintenance. This organisation offers such owners the option of subscribing to a yearly check-up of their building. Monument Watch inspects the building and the owner receives a report on its technical state and can then decide whether to restore, repair or maintain the monument. The reports are accepted by the Department for Conservation as technical proof of the need for grant assistance when an application for a grant is received. The Department actually provides part of the finance for the operation of the Monument Watch service. Financial assistance can also be given to pay for at least part of the cost of the Monument Watch report (the full amount in the case of churches).

iii. Subsidies for country houses

Grant aid is provided for protected historic country seats, allowing the owner to apply for payment for the maintenance of objects situated in the grounds, for example, garden vases, bridges, hen houses and other objects intended for decoration of the grounds, or buildings with a functional use, like a hothouse. The main building and outhouses are excluded from this regulation. For the maintenance of 'green' elements of a country seat, a grant can be asked from the Ministry of Agriculture.

iv. Other grants

A number of subsidies have been occasionally provided for special purposes, for example to pay for the restoration of damage to stone-work or metalwork caused by acid rain. Also there have been large grants for major restoration work to churches, castles and windmills, where costs were more than €500 000.

3.3.7. United States of America (USA)

Funding assistance for historic buildings in the USA is now more directed through tax incentive measures, but some grant aid has been maintained.

The US Department of the Interior, through the National Park Service (NPS), administers the Federal Historic Preservation Fund Grants in Aid Program. This programme provides federal funding to states and terri-tories for preservation activities. To ensure state and local commitment to heritage projects, all grants are 50:50 matching grants. Recipients may provide matching funds in the form of services in kind (including supplies, developing photographs, office rent and administrative costs), cash or volunteer hours. All grant-aided work must be carried out in accordance with the Secretary of Interior's *Standards for Historic Preservation*, under the guidance and supervision of the State Historic Preservation Officer.

4. Loan and credit facilities

4.0. Introduction

All credit activities are strictly regulated to protect consumers. Such regulation sets the limits imposed on the granting of loans, particularly those backed by the consumer's own funds.

Specialist lending institutions play a role in providing property loans and, with more countries in Europe moving towards market-based economies and greater deregulation, there are greater opportunities for lending activity associated with property. However, some credit institutions may be less willing to invest in old buildings (which may involve higher repair costs and less flexibility compared to modern buildings and therefore may pose a greater credit risk).

As credit institutions usually base their lending on appraisal of the risks to be incurred, there may be a lack of interest in supporting repair, restoration or rehabilitation activity as it is not always clear to what extent such investment will increase the value of property. Therefore it may be necessary to introduce measures to cover or diminish the risks in order to encourage credit institutions to finance old buildings, particularly by combining mortgage loans with public subsidies, establishing appropriate forms of insurance and providing security backed by public authorities (central or local government).

Diminishing risks can be achieved, for example, by means of a public guarantee. In order to realise their commitment to enhance the heritage, authorities could also participate in joint structures involving a number of partners and aimed at handling rehabilitation programmes.

Public authorities may provide credit through loans or loan guarantees as a way to encourage funding for architectural heritage conservation. Direct government loans, funded from the treasury or state finance department, will be serviced by the government (collecting scheduled repayments from the borrowers). When central or local government guarantees a loan, a private lender, such as a commercial bank, originates the loan, secures the government guarantee and services the loan. The government enters into a contractual agreement to make full or partial payment to the lender if the borrower defaults on the loan.

Credit programmes are attractive tools for policymakers who want to serve constituents who may not be eligible for grant aid. If loans are intended to help a borrower to repair, restore or rehabilitate property, they generally will be secured loans. Loan terms (such as the loan amount, fees, interest rates, maturities and conditions of default) vary. By extending credit through targeted credit programmes to disadvantaged but creditworthy borrowers, the government can demonstrate to private lenders that those borrowers are profitable credit risks.

The choice between direct loans and loan guarantees involves political considerations. Private financial institutions are a powerful constituency that favour loan guarantees rather than direct loans, because this avoids the threat of direct government participation in the credit business.

Examples of credit and loan facilities for architectural heritage can be seen in a number of countries.

4.1. Denmark

In Denmark, the State Preservation of Buildings Fund can provide low-interest loans (1% below normal bank rates) for preservation work to listed buildings. As the subsidies offered in Denmark can be in the form of a grant or a low-interest loan, owners can decide on the most beneficial form of financial support for them. In periods of low interest rates and fiscal expansion, owners will generally prefer grant aid because it represents money in their pocket that does not have to be repaid. A top-up loan can be combined with a grant to fund the balance of costs. The loan option will only be popular during periods of high interest rates and monetary restraint, when owners have difficulty getting loans from mortgage institutions. Loans of up to 90% of the market value of the property are provided, with a payback period of up to 30 years through annual instalments.

Apart from listed buildings, other buildings that are "worthy of preservation" and rural housing can be supported by public-sector loans. The Building Repair Committee Programme (Bygningsforbedringsudvalg) supports the repair and conservation of buildings (mainly external works). Depending on their ability to match state funds, local authorities may establish a special committee incorporating representatives of the local authority, owners of houses, tenants and preservation organisations. Each local authority can decide independently how much state-allocated funding is transferred to the committee. Following application by the owner, the committee decides whether they will finance projects via an interest-free loan, up to a maximum of two thirds of the cost of eligible works, such as external works to façades, roofs and windows. Once set up, the committee has complete autonomy in allocation of funds. The local authority has no influence in committee decisions. The installation of modern facilities, such as kitchens or toilets, is not eligible for funding. Monthly capital and interest repayments do not have to be made unless the property is sold, in which case the loans must be repaid in full.

In addition, the Renovation of Buildings Programme (Bygningsfornyelse) has provided financial support for major repairs and improvements to residential buildings (including buildings "worthy of preservation"). A percentage of the financial loss to the owner of residential improvements is grant-aided by the state and the balance is provided in the form of a low-interest loan. For example, 30% of the cost will be given in the form of a grant and the balance as a loan. The actual percentage varies with the level of rent charged to tenants (particularly low-income earners) after completion of improvement works.

4.2. Netherlands

The Nationaal Restauratiefonds was set up in the Netherlands in 1985 because there were insufficient resources available for restoration. It works as a revolving fund, issuing loans at reduced interest rates, usually 5% below normal bank rates (recently as low as 1%), with the loan acting like a mortgage by being spread over a long time (a minimum of 10 years and usually up to 30 years). The loan is offered for the non-subsidised costs of a project and is guaranteed by local authorities. The rate of interest is fixed over the period of the loan and there are no charges for early repayment (see section 2.4.2).

4.3. United Kingdom

The Architectural Heritage Fund was set up in 1975 to support work on historic buildings, particularly those that might not benefit from grant aid. Its principal activity is to support the work of building preservation trusts, of which there are now nearly 200, spread throughout the United Kingdom. The fund provides grants for feasibility studies, project administration, project organisers and (refundable) project development grants, but most significantly it offers low-interest loans (see sections 2.1.2 and 2.4, and Figure 1).

If a building preservation trust intends to apply for a loan and/or expects to borrow money from a bank, it will need to offer security for the amount borrowed. The fund may require a first charge (a mortgage) over the building for whose repair the loan is required and this charge may be extended to cover any building that a trust owns. Otherwise a formal guarantee of repayment may be required from a bank, a local authority or comparable corporate body. The value of the mortgaged property must not be less than 70% of the sum loaned. Also, to qualify for a loan the trust must have charitable status (be set up for the non-profit activity of repairing/rehabilitating a historic building). Trusts can apply for up to 75% of the gross estimated cost of the project, which may include purchase of the property, repair, conservation and altera-tion to enable a new beneficial use (subject to necessary consents).

4.4. USA

The United States Federal Government can guarantee up to 90% of the principal sum offered on loans made by private lenders for works to properties that are designated historic structures and have been placed on the National Register. The rehabilitation of historic buildings for affordable housing can also benefit from subsidised loans or direct subsidies made by the Federal Home Loan Bank.

The Federal Government may also provide a federal tax exemption for debt obligations issued by state or local governments, such as the financing of preservation programmes through the issuing of bonds (see section 2.6). Bond issues back many state tax-credit initiatives for programmes through the state bond bank. By pooling the credit standing of participating local governments, the bond bank permits local governments to borrow at a lower cost or on more favourable terms than they could otherwise.

A number of revolving preservation funds have been established to provide low-interest loans for the rehabilitation of historic property (see section 2.4).

Discriminatory practice by some lending institutions in the United States resulted in credit being denied to creditworthy applicants and this was found to contribute to the physical and economic demise of low-income historic areas. Legislation on the provision of mortgages for the purchase of homes has required commercial lenders to provide an annual statement, in an effort to assess the lenders' efforts to meet local credit needs and encourage innovative partnerships with community groups and local governments. This legislation has been used by heritage foundations to negotiate loans from commercial banks for historic property.

Other examples of low-interest lending are found in revolving funds and various schemes to support action on old buildings (see sections 2.4 and 2.6 for the Netherlands, the UK and the USA, and section 6.2.3 for historic districts and towns in France).

5. Fiscal measures to benefit heritage conservation

5.0. Introduction

The Council of Europe's report *New Ways of Funding the Restoration of the Architectural Heritage* (1988), following the Messina Colloquy, and its 1991 publication *Funding the Architectural Heritage* showed that the special quality of architectural heritage fully justifies the provision of special tax incentives. Furthermore, the Council of Europe Recommendation No. R (91) 6 of the Committee of Ministers to member states on measures likely to promote the funding of the conservation of the architectural heritage indicated that measures should be taken, particularly in countries where the tax system favours investment in new rather than old buildings, to arrive at a situation where taxation provisions encourage conservation, maintenance, restoration and rehabilitation of old buildings.

Taxation measures and regulations can prevent owners and potential investors in heritage property from investing in what could otherwise be profitable and beneficial for architectural heritage. The rationale for policy makers using tax incentives as a tool in heritage conservation is the idea that it is less coercive than direct government action such as regulation or grant subsidies. It allows more freedom of choice to take action, which in theory should lead to more efficient economic outcomes.

Tax-based incentives involve no direct transfer of money, although foregone taxes represent a cost to the state budget and therefore to a nation as a whole. However, activities benefiting from the incentive will usually create tax revenues, from employment in conservation and restoration work, business occupation of premises and so on. Such incentives can used to encourage action on architectural heritage in broadly three ways:

- incentives to reduce the cost of conservation, maintenance, restoration and rehabilitation;
- incentives to prevent the demolition and replacement of architectural heritage assets in favour of redevelopment;

- incentives to encourage sponsorship and donations to non-profit organisations such as foundations and other heritage organisations that will take action on heritage property.

As taxation is usually the sole responsibility of a particular government ministry, department or agency dealing with tax revenue, tax incentives will largely be determined by the relevant taxation authority, whereas subsidies and loans are more likely to be controlled by the competent heritage authority. The relevant authority should inform the public about the availability of tax incentives, and issue regulations and explanatory notes to ensure equitable distribution of the incentive. It may also be necessary to issue internal interpretive regulations to enable public officials such as heritage officials to determine eligibility for incentives.

Different forms of tax incentives can be considered, including income or profits tax, value added tax on the sale of goods and services (including maintenance or restoration works), inheritance and capital transfer tax, and property or land (occupation) taxes.

5.1. Forms of tax incentives

5.1.1. Income tax incentives

There are two forms of income-tax-based incentives for work on heritage property:
- tax deductions (relief), where the owner may deduct specified expenditure from income, reducing effective taxable income, subject to limits;
- tax credits, where the owner may deduct a fixed percentage of specified expenditure from income tax payable.

In tax deductions, the benefit received by the owner is a direct result of his/her marginal rate of tax liability. Thus, the incentive is regressive because the tax benefit rises with the income of the recipient (if there are different income tax rates). A tax credit is more equitable as it offers the same percentage allowance on all expenditures.

One problem associated with income tax incentives is that people earning low incomes may not benefit form the provisions. However, as a matter of public policy, some countries such as the United Kingdom and the United States provide refundable monetary payments in the form of "tax credits" targeted at individuals on low incomes. Although these are unrelated to heritage conservation, they show that tax expenditure could be directed for this purpose to ensure that all individuals could benefit from tax incentives. The approach adopted in western European countries tends to favour deducting eligible expenditure from income (the exception being Spain), whereas in the United States a tax credit system is in operation.

Some tax incentive systems may be targeted for the dual purpose of safeguarding heritage property and providing social benefits, such as rented housing for people on low incomes. Although there are few such systems in operation, this has been identified as a goal of integrated conservation mechanisms by the Council of Europe (see section 5.2.3).

5.2. Income tax cost-deduction systems

The general approach for this type of incentive is for eligible costs to relate to approved conservation or restoration, but not improvement work. However, in some instances a wider range of rehabilitation works may benefit. Some examples follow.

5.2.1. Belgium

According to the Belgian Income Tax Code, owners of classified architectural monuments are allowed to deduct non-subsidised maintenance and restoration costs (any cost not covered by grant aid) for residential owner-occupiers (rented property does not benefit) up to a specified limit. The regional heritage authority must first determine the work needed and its standard. The owner must then incur the expenditure before claiming the tax rebate; payment depends on the work being satisfactory. Furthermore, the owner is usually required to allow public access for a number of days per year for up to 10 years if elements of the building that have benefited from the incentive are not visible from the exterior or street level. Protected sites, rather than individually protected monuments, do not benefit from this incentive.

5.2.2. Denmark

In Denmark, a special income-tax relief system has assisted private owners of listed houses (which include all listed buildings in other uses that were originally constructed as houses). This system was negotiated by the Danish Association of Owners of Historic Houses (Bygnings Frednings Foreningen or BYFO) and is embedded in tax legislation. BYFO is an independent non-profit organisation administered by two qualified restoration architects, a tax specialist and an executive assistant. In order to qualify for the incentive, private owners must subscribe to the organisation through an annual membership fee. BYFO administers the system itself, which greatly reduces administration and bureaucracy by the local tax authority. The tax authority also benefits because maintenance expenditure creates increased income tax from organisations and individuals employed on maintenance work and increased VAT revenue from the supply of materials and services. The Danish government originally authorised the system because it would increase tax revenue from historic houses in private ownership.

The incentive is designed to encourage owners to maintain their properties (but it does not apply to improvement costs). It is a formula-based system of assessment termed "decay per annum" based on an assessment of elements of the building (external walls, external and internal materials, service installations and other aspects) and a figure representing the rate of decay for the entire building; each element will have its own lifespan and cost figure, which is updated annually by a building cost index. For example, if roof tiles cost €10 per square metre and would normally have a life of 35 years, for 100 sq. m of roof area the figure for the roof element would be 100 × 10 ÷ 35, or about €28.

The "decay per annum" amount is the total figure for all elements considered in the survey of the building. It shows the total decay amount for the entire building, not for the individual elements of the building. Owners may choose to write off substantial maintenance expenditure against income tax in two ways. First, owners may spend a large sum on maintenance and deduct the decay per annum rate in the current and subsequent years. It is, however, more common for owners to wait until an adequate decay per annum rate has accumulated over a number of years so the full expenditure can be deducted immediately. The tax deduction is allowed whether or not the works are carried out – it is provided as an incentive to encourage maintenance.

The decay per annum report can transfer from one owner to another, but any maintenance expenditure in excess of the total decay amount cannot be transferred to a new owner upon sale of a protected structure. Upon transfer of ownership, the accumulated decay per annum is forfeited and the "tax meter" begins again with the new owner.

5.2.3. France

In France a number of general tax incentives are available to owners of non-historical property with respect to income derived from the property. Different rules apply depending whether a building is rented or owner-occupied. For rented property, eligible expenses incurred from letting (such as administration costs, caretaker costs, insurance premiums, property taxes, certain maintenance, repair, renovation and improvement costs) may be deducted from the income received in the form of rent. If these deductions result in a deficit, it can be carried over to income derived from the property (not overall income) for the following 10 years. For owner-occupied property, the owner may not deduct any expenses from income, but a tax reduction (credit) has been available for eligible repairs and improvements.

Apart from the general tax incentives for property, a special tax system applies to specified protected or certified historic buildings. These include "classified historic monuments", monuments listed with the title of "historic monument" and other "certified buildings" (buildings considered as belonging to the heritage because of their special historic, artistic or tourist interest and certified as such by the Ministry of Economic Affairs and Finance). This special tax system applies to all parts of an architectural complex, not just those parts that are classified, listed or certified, if they constitute an indivisible whole as far as the protection of relevant parts are concerned.

Different rules apply to rented protected buildings and non-rented protected buildings, and for the latter whether they are open to the public or not. The deductible amount must not include the cost of any work that has been otherwise subsidised. The deductibility of expenditure on monuments depends on whether the monument is open to the public. Opening to the public is not mandatory under French law, but only 50% of eligible expenses can be deducted from total revenue if public access is not allowed for a specified number of days per year.

The owners of buildings that are not classified as historic monuments or listed with the title of historic monument, but have been specially certified because of their historic or artistic characteristics, may also benefit from reduced income tax based on losses incurred in respect of the property. However, only half the amount of any eligible expenditure on the property is deductible from taxable income, even if the building is open to the public.

The rules for owners of buildings that are classified, listed or certified (as above) are as follows:

- If the whole building is rented, the owner may deduct all property-related expenses (subject to general law tax provisions as above, but any deficit may be carried over to overall income). Property-related expenses include costs in relation to upkeep of the monument and amounts paid as contributions to any work carried out by the state or the proportion of expenses actually borne by the owner in the event of subsidised work being carried out.

- If the building is occupied or partially occupied by the owner (and is not rented), a distinction is made between buildings which are the source of supplementary income through entrance fees for opening the property to the public and those which are not. If there are no receipts from entry fees (the building is closed, or open to the public free of charge), the situation is similar to that of a rented building (costs can be deducted from overall income). If a supplementary income is obtained from entry fees, further deductions can be made from the owner's income raised from the property.

Tax incentives are also provided in relation to the expenses derived and costs incurred (for purchasing, renting, or maintaining) from using a classified historic monument, a monument listed with the title of historic monument or a certified property for commercial purposes.

Further income tax incentives exist for rented residential property in a *secteur sauvegardé* (conservation area) or a zone of architectural, urban and landscape importance (ZZAUP – see also section 2.2.1). Tax incentives are designed to promote collective property restructuring schemes in these designated areas through building works and to help boost the market for rented residential accommodation. Owners may deduct loan interest and expenditure incurred for maintenance, repair and improvement works (as defined under ordinary rules) as well as other approved costs (see below) from rental income derived from residential property. Any resulting deficit for property tax purposes may be deducted from the landlord's total taxable income so long as the owner has leased the restored property, unfurnished, as a tenant's main residence and the length of tenancy is at least six years. No maximum limit applies. Since 1995, eligibility for tax relief has been restricted to:

- restoration work in a *secteur sauvegardé* where a conservation and enhancement plan (PSMV) has been approved (this tax break applies from the date the PSMV is published);
- restoration work in an established *secteur sauvegardé* before the creation of a PSMV where a declaration of public interest for property restoration has been made for eligible works, or in a designated ZPPAUP, provided that the restoration work is carried out within a "property restoration perimeter" and has been declared to be of public interest.

Deductible expenses can include any necessary work for the conversion of property to residential use where this has been approved by the official architect (Architecte des Bâtiments de France). Demolition work may also be tax-deductible if it is a compulsory part of the competent authorities' planning permission and if it is specified in a conservation and enhancement plan or in a declaration that the restoration work is of public interest. Where demolition makes it necessary to re-roof existing buildings or rebuild their external walls, this work also is tax-deductible. New building, rebuilding and extensions are not deductible. To be eligible for tax relief, projects must be carried out by a member of one of these groups:

- private landlords, including individual owners, associations of owners or an investment company;
- public authorities (including government planning bodies), semi-public companies contracted or licensed to run a project, or low-cost housing associations authorised to carry out restoration work;
- non-profit associations set up to carry out housing improvement or restoration.

Rehabilitation work carried out by owners within a property restoration perimeter can take advantage of special tax deductions, including deductions from property and income taxes, if they undertake to lease the buildings as unfurnished dwellings for a minimum period of six years and the lease commences within 12 months after the completion of the property restoration works (see Figures 10 and 11). It has been proposed to increase the minimum lease period to at least nine years.

5.2.4. Germany

Tax incentives are used in a variety of ways in Germany to preserve, improve and rehabilitate historic property.

Maintenance and other expenditure (such as utility improvements) on an existing building (whether a protected building or not) up to a specified limit is tax-deductible in Germany. In the case of protected property (whether single or part of an ensemble) both maintenance and rehabilitation costs are given specific tax incentives. In relation to maintenance expenses, the situation depends on whether the property generates an income and whether the building is owner-occupied or leased.

i. Properties not generating income (and the owner does not live in the building)

Owners can deduct maintenance and repair costs from their taxable income over a 10-year period at a rate of 10% from the year in which the expense was first incurred. The work must have been deemed necessary and approved in advance by the relevant department of cultural affairs. No income must have been derived from the building during the year in which the expenses were incurred (such as entrance fees to castles or palaces in private ownership).

Types of eligible expenditure include the renewal of existing parts of the building, such as repair work, exterior rendering, external cladding, heating or sanitary installations.

ii. Properties not generating income (the property is owner-occupied)

Protected buildings that are occupied by the owner (and buildings otherwise certified by the municipal authority as being of historic, artistic or cultural interest) are given the same deduction allowance as in point i. above. This provides a significant incentive because other non-protected or non-certified old buildings are only entitled to an allowance of €1 278 per year over an eight-year period, provided that the income does not exceed a defined limit.

iii. Properties generating income (e.g. from entrance fees)

The tax authorities treat any expenditure on general upkeep not in excess of €2 000 as routine maintenance and tax-deductible.

iv. Properties earning a rent derived from a lease

Owners of protected or certified buildings that are leased can spread deduction of maintenance expenses over two to five years. This gives a definite advantage over other buildings where such expenses are only deductible from rental income for the year when they were incurred.

There is also "accelerated depreciation" of rehabilitation expenses for tax purposes, benefiting protected and certified buildings (and buildings in urban areas designated for rehabilitation). Rehabilitation of a protected building for a new use, such as a former factory or agricultural building, can benefit from the tax incentive if the historical substance of the building is preserved (or the works are such that the building could revert to its historical design).

In Germany in certain circumstances the purchase costs of buying an architectural monument for use (to achieve a taxable income) can also be deducted from income tax. This incentive is used to reflect the loss of value compared to buying a non-protected property and is designed to encourage investment in protected buildings.

5.2.5. Ireland

Section 482 of the Irish Taxes Consolidation Act 1997 enables private owner-occupiers of buildings and gardens that have been identified as "intrinsically of significant architectural, historical, scientific, horticultural or aesthetic interest" (depending on whether it is a building or garden or both) to offset the cost of repair, maintenance or restoration of the property against income or corporation tax liability. Additional relief, up to an aggregate of €6 350, is provided for repair, maintenance or restoration of approved objects in an approved property if the objects are on display for a period of at least two years from the year in which the expenditure is claimed, for the installation, maintenance or replacement of a security alarm system and for the cost of public liability insurance.

To qualify for the relief, the Revenue Commissioners must be satisfied that public access to the whole or a substantial part of the property is afforded for a period of at least 60 days in any one year, including not less than 40 days in the period 1 May to 30 September inclusive, for at least four hours per day, and that any admission price is reasonable.

This provision does not apply to all protected structures (for which limited grant aid is provided), only those properties that have been identified by the Minister for Arts, Heritage, Gaeltacht and the Islands as having the required interest. The range of eligible buildings includes castles, churches, larger houses and some 18th-century town houses.

By May 2004, a total of 445 properties had been approved under the scheme since it began in 1982. However, this figure includes many properties that had been listed in previous years and only 166 properties were eligible for this relief at this date.

5.2.6. Italy

The provision of tax incentives depends on whether buildings have been recognised as being of special cultural interest under a decree issued by the Ministry of Cultural Affairs or whether they qualify as being part of the national historic and artistic heritage. Owners of protected buildings can offset repair and maintenance costs against income tax, but with different rules applying in relation to rented and non-rented property and geographical location.

i. Non-rented properties

Owners of protected buildings are permitted to deduct 19% of the repair and maintenance costs from their income tax liability. The deduction of costs is, however, only allowed where the Ministry of Cultural Affairs has certified the necessity of the expenditure.

ii. Rented properties

In the case of rented property, maintenance expenses are deducted from rental income (not the gross tax). A flat rate equivalent to 15% of the rent (or rateable value if higher) applies and the owner cannot make any other deductions. Higher rates are available in certain places. The flat rate deduction is 25% for properties in central Venice or on the islands of Giudecca, Murano and Burano; in places where rental levels are high (in particular, Bologna, Florence, Genoa, Milan, Naples, Palermo, Rome, Turin and Venice and their suburbs), owners are entitled to a further 30% deduction (in addition to the 15 or 25%).

5.2.7. Netherlands

Owners of state-level protected historic buildings can offset all repair and maintenance works against income tax, and improvements such as provision of kitchen and bathroom facilities, plumbing and heating. Owners of historic monuments protected at provincial or municipal level are not able to use the income tax deduction.

5.3. Tax credit systems

Tax credit incentives are not widely used in Europe, but have a significant role in the United States of America.

5.3.1. Spain

An example of a European country using a tax credit system of incentives is Spain. Owners of properties that have been included in the General Register of Properties of Cultural Interest are entitled to claim tax credits. Owners are allowed a tax credit equivalent to 15% of any expenditure incurred on conservation, repair and restoration works, provided that the building is opened to the public and the sum incurred has not already been deducted from property income for tax purposes.

5.3.2. USA

In the USA the Federal Historic Rehabilitation Income Tax Credit rewards private investment in rehabilitating historic properties that are depreciable buildings in office, commercial, industrial or agricultural use or for rental housing (owners of owner-occupied houses cannot benefit from this incentive). Two forms of tax credit are provided:

- a 20% tax credit for the certified rehabilitation of certified historic structures;
- a 10% tax credit for the rehabilitation of non-historic, non-residential buildings built before 1936.

A building eligible for the 20% tax credit must be either a certified historic structure listed individually in the National Register of Historic Places or a building in a Registered Historic District and certified as contributing to the historic significance of the Registered Historic District (see Figure 12). Buildings designated at state or local level will also be considered as Certified Historic Structures if the designation is certified as conforming to the National Register criteria. Projects undertaken for the 10% tax credit must meet physical requirements for retention of external walls and the internal structural framework.

The approval process for the 20% tax credit requires submission of a three-part Historic Preservation Certification to ensure that works confirm with the Secretary of the Interior's Standards for Rehabilitation. If a rehabilitated property is disposed of within five years of being placed back in use the tax credit will be recaptured on a sliding scale at 20% per annum over the five years.

In addition to the federal tax credit, some state heritage programmes administer income tax credits that supplement the federal system or do something similar for historic properties that are certified as historic structures at state or municipal level but are not entitled to federal tax incentives. Some of these state tax credits apply to owner-occupied houses. For example, North Carolina offers some of the most generous tax incentives for preservation in the USA, with rehabilitation tax credits of 20% for commercial property owners and 30% for owner occupied historic dwellings. The 20% commercial tax credit can be added to the federal tax credit of 20% to provide a combined credit of 40%.

Tax incentives: Federal Historic Rehabilitation Tax Credit, USA

This complex of buildings constructed 1885-1891 for the Reading Rail-road Company as offices and an arcade were originally part of a larger complex of building linked to the market and train shed. It is certified in the National Register of Historic Places in the USA and rehabilitated to provide a mixed use of retail, restaurant and hotel functions. The rehabilitation work involved restoration of original storefronts, external re-pointing and a new roof, as well as interior works to restore original works including metal ceilings and plaster finishes, the division of the upper floor into hotel rooms and the provision of new entrances, and the installation of elevators and escalators. The rehabilitation costs eligible for the Federal Historic Rehabilitation Tax Credit amounted to US $72 313 171 providing a tax credit (20%) of US $14 462 634. To qualify for the tax credit the rehabilitation had to comply with the Secretary of the Interior's Standards for Rehabilitation and Guidelines for Rehabilitating Historic Buildings.

Figure 12 – Market Street Façade of the Reading Railway Terminal Headhouse, Philadelphia, a beneficiary of the Federal Historic Rehabilitation Tax Credit

5.3.3. Tax credits for rehabilitation of social housing

In the USA, the Federal Rehabilitation Tax Credit can be combined with an investment tax credit for the acquisition, construction, or rehabilitation of low-income housing for occupants who meet specific income requirements. An existing building does not need to be a certified historic structure to quality for the low-income housing tax credit. However, where a certified historic structure is rehabilitated for use as low income housing, the combination of the rehabilitation tax credit (as above) and the low-income housing tax credit (as below) provides more capital for rehabilitation projects, ensuring that historic buildings are preserved and for a socially useful purpose.

In a historic rehabilitation project that will be used for low-income housing, the rehabilitation cost on which the low-income housing credit is based is reduced by the amount of the historic rehabilitation credit. There are two housing tax credit percentages that apply to buildings that qualify as "substantially rehabilitated":

- a 70% tax credit for rehabilitation expenditure that has not been federally subsidised, equating to a credit of about 9% per annum for 10 years; and

- a 30% tax credit for rehabilitation expenditure that has been federally subsidised (by grant aid), equating to a credit of about 4% per annum for 10 years.

These levels can be increased for the rehabilitation of buildings in designated difficult development areas.

The low-income housing tax credit is available for a 10-year period (see Figure 13). To gain the full credit, a housing project must set aside a minimum percentage of rent-restricted units that meet certain criteria for cost per unit and income of occupants relative to area median incomes, and it must remain in compliance with the occupant's income limits for 15 years. Failure to comply with the rent-restriction requirements over this period results in a recapture of a portion of the credit plus interest.

This system of tax credits in the USA has been found to be very effective in encouraging investment in rehabilitation projects. The possibility of combining two forms of tax credit can be critical to the financial viability of rehabilitation projects.

Developers can entice investors into rehabilitation projects by, in effect, selling the benefit of the tax credit. A typical approach is to form a limited partnership, with the project sponsor as general partner (see section 2.3). Investors buy into the partnership as limited partners by making capital contributions to cover project costs. Each partner's share of the profits and losses for tax purposes is based on the partner's share in the partnership. In order to provide a return on the investment to the investor-partners, the investment in the partnership is less than the amount of the credit itself.

Furthermore, non-profit organisations can buy historic buildings and syndicate the restoration project by forming a limited partnership, where the non-profit agency holds a 1% interest in the property as a limited partner and the syndicate holds the other 99%. The non-profit organisation ensures that the building is rehabilitated and the investors receive the passive benefit of the tax credit. Ownership of the historic building reverts back to the non-profit organisation once the tax credits have been received by the passive syndicate members and the recapture period has elapsed.

Tax incentives for rehabilitation as social housing, USA

Project financing for No. 210 Academy Road, Trenton, New Jersey, USA:

Costs eligible for the federal historic rehabilitation tax credit:	$ 253 700
Less tax credit @ 20%	$ 50 740
Costs eligible for low-income housing tax credit	$ 202 960
Tax credit @ 9% per annum	$ 18 266

Total tax credit

Low income tax credit over 10 years:	$ 182 660
Historic rehabilitation tax credit	$ 50 740
Total credit	$ 233 400

*Figure 13 – "Brownstone" houses circa 1900 situated in
the Academy Hanover Historic District in Trenton, New Jersey.*

Nos. 210, 212 and 214 Academy Road were rehabilitated by converting each single residence into two low-income residential units with the benefit of both the 20% Federal Historic Rehabilitation Tax Credit and low-income housing tax credit.

5.3.4. Tax credits in Canada

The Federal Tax Law for Canada does not provide specific incentives in support of preserving historic buildings. In fact, property owners are given encouragement to demolish buildings by being able to write off 75% of the depreciated value of a building against income tax. There has been criticism that Canada has lost more than 20% of its pre-1920 heritage buildings over the last thirty or so years, and this has led to calls to reverse the situation. The Historic Places Initiative of 2001 set out a national strategy for the conservation of historic places, with a vision of encouraging partnerships between governments, communities and the private sector, including the use of tax credits ands grant funding programmes. But, owing to budget cuts, this programme ended in 2006. Pressure remains, though, particularly from the Heritage Canada Foundation, to introduce tax credits similar to those in the USA.

5.4. Property tax incentives

Property taxes are normally levied on the market rental or capital value of a property for the purpose of raising municipal revenue. There can also be a tax on the purchase of property.

Property tax incentives take different forms, such as an assessment freeze, a current-use assessment (as opposed to alternative, best economic use), assessment as a percentage of full market value, reduced rates of property tax (for historic buildings) or complete exemption. These forms of relief, which may be temporary or permanent, can be aimed at alleviating the high expenditure and rising property values that can be a result of heritage conservation (where conservation work leads to an improvement in the property and so may cause an increase in property assessment/value, with a resulting increase in taxation). Despite the potential for an increased tax base in the long term, many authorities are reluctant to initiate property tax rebates on the renovation of historic buildings because they fear short-term revenue losses.

Property taxes are often punitive and thus a disincentive to conservation work on heritage structures, because such work may increase the property value and so increase the tax due. To alleviate this problem, property tax incentives can encourage action on heritage assets.

Here follow some examples of property tax incentives in different countries.

5.4.1. Belgium

In the Brussels-Capital region of Belgium, the regional government exempts from the property tax (assessed annually on immovable property) any classified property that is not let or in use. By contrast, in the

Flemish region of Belgium the City of Bruges municipal authority has taken action to reduce the level of vacant and neglected buildings by imposing a punitive accumulative tax on owners (see Figure 14). The tax is calculated by the metre, for example, a gable of 10 m will have a tax liability of €2 500 in the first year. This is doubled in the second year if the owner does not take remedial action. The accumulated tax is then given to the Social Impulse Foundation (SIF) to fight against building neglect.

Subsidies and punitive tax measures, Bruges, Belgium

In mid 1980s the City of Bruges municipal authority started to buy derelict historic houses and restore them in order to provide an exemplar. After restoration these houses were sold or rented out to interested young families. At the same time the municipal authority tried to incite private investors to take necessary initiatives for restoring the many derelict dwellings throughout the city. The decision-makers established a system of subsidies, starting with architectural repairs, which received a subsidy of up to 60% and a lump sum for the improvement of sewage, kitchen and bathroom amenities. This decision led to significant improvements to the traditional building stock in the city. A further way of encouraging action to reduce the number of vacant and neglected buildings was by the introduction of the punitive accumulative tax on owners.

Figure 14 – Historic houses in Bruges, Belgium restored and rehabilitated through a combination of financial assistance and punitive tax measures.

5.4.2. Denmark

In Denmark, owners of listed property are exempt from estate tax on property if they sign a special preservation declaration foregoing their right to demand that the state government purchase the property in the event of a refusal to allow demolition. In theory, the tax saving can fund maintenance of listed buildings, though there is no guarantee that this saving will be expended on maintenance (but owners of listed houses are given encouragement to maintain them through the "decay per annum" income tax incentive: see section 5.2.2). This relief is beneficial to owners in urban areas where land values are high (but is less relevant in rural areas where rates are comparatively low).

5.4.3. France

There are no specific reductions in property tax for historic buildings in France (apart from certain properties that have the "label" of the Fondation du Patrimoine; see section 2.2.1). But, if a building's repair costs are particularly high, its assessed value may be lowered to reduce its owner's wealth tax liability.

5.4.4. Germany

In Germany, municipal authorities give property tax exemption to owners of protected buildings because their safeguarding is regarded as being in the public interest. This exemption applies as long as any income derived from a building is lower than the costs relating to its upkeep (so they are a source of recurring loss). The property must also have been used for cultural purposes and have been in the same family ownership for over 20 years.

5.4.5. Ireland

All residential property is exempt from rates (property tax) in Ireland. However, no property tax concession exists specifically for protected structures, though unoccupied commercial property is exempt from commercial property rates, subject to the ratepayer providing proof (such as newspaper advertisements) of attempts to let the property.

5.4.6. Italy

In Italy, all owners of buildings are deemed to receive property income, even where they do not lease the property concerned. The income is calculated on the basis of the average rateable value. Municipal property tax is payable annually at a rate which varies between 4 and 7% depending on the municipality concerned, and the tax base is proportional to the property's rateable value. In the case of protected buildings, the rateable value applied is the lowest for the land register area in which the property is located.

5.4.7. Spain

In Spain, historical and artistic monuments specifically declared to be "properties of cultural value" are exempt from payment of urban and rural annual levies collected by municipalities.

5.4.8. United Kingdom

In England, unoccupied listed buildings, buildings subject to a preservation notice and scheduled monuments eligible for commercial use are exempt from the uniform business rate (a form of property tax based on the rental value of the property). This provision was designed to help owners not receiving an income from a property to take action to maintain it.

5.4.9. USA

In the USA, the property tax system assesses the value of the underlying land of historic structures as well as the value of the improvements to the property. Where a heritage building is in an area zoned for high-rise construction, the development potential of the land beneath the building may exceed the market value of the existing structure. However, various property tax incentives have been designed to encourage action on historic buildings.

For example, a property tax abatement programme in Washington State excludes any increase in value, from residential and commercial building rehabilitation, over its assessed property tax value for 10 years – subject to the work following national rehabilitation standards and a public access requirement once a year. In North Carolina, locally designated structures receive a 50% reduction in property tax. State enabling legislation gives Maryland's local governments the option to set up rehabilitation property tax credit programmes within locally designated historic districts. There are two options. The first option is a property tax credit allowing property owners in historic districts to deduct 10% of their rehabilitation expenditure from the property tax. The second option freezes property tax at pre-rehabilitation level for a period of 10 years. A number of states (such as Maryland, New Jersey, New York and Texas) have also passed legislation to give property tax exemptions and credits to "qualified organisations" such as historical societies, non-profit organisations, government agencies, educational organisations and archaeological societies that are stewards or owners of historic property.

5.4.10. Canada

In Canada, the property tax burden as a percentage of market value is less for vacant land than it is for existing commercial or residential buildings. Thus, the relationship between market demand, land use planning/zoning and the property tax assessment system gives owners an incentive to demolish their buildings to avoid the tax burden of retaining heritage buildings. Moreover, tax revenue valuations do not recognise the excess costs associated with the repair of historic structures or the fact that, when a building owner makes substantial expenditure for repair and rehabilitation, this may even increase the value for tax purposes. An example to combat this problem is indicated by a municipal property tax rebate system offered by the City of Edmonton, Alberta. Owners of designated heritage properties may be considered for three levels of compensation on the basis that:

- a building's tax assessment may encourage demolition rather than rehabilitation;

- cash flow may be restricted during rehabilitation;

- owners may be penalised for rehabilitation through increased property taxes relative to the improved market value following rehabilitation.

Level 1 Compensation was developed in response to situations where a building's tax assessment encourages property owners to demolish heritage buildings to use the site as a car park. A rebate of the portion of property taxes relating to the building is provided for up to five years. Property tax on the land element must continue to be paid in full. In essence, the property owner is paying property tax for a vacant site while the building is still there. This protects the building from demolition but it does not encourage rehabilitation.

Level 2 Compensation was developed to alleviate the problem of restricted cash flow to heritage property owners during rehabilitation, by giving a two-year rebate on building and land tax assessments.

Level 3 Compensation was introduced to prevent a situation where property owners would be penalised for rehabilitating a heritage property by the fact that the property tax assessment would increase substantially because of the higher market value of the property after rehabilitation. Any increase in property tax liability after rehabilitation is offset by a reducing level of rebate over five years, after which the building owner reverts to paying full property taxes. In effect, the City rebates the incremental tax portion (see Figure 15).

Level 3 Alternative Compensation (Level 3A) was developed to give the City the option to pay for the restoration of architecturally significant portions of a building (see Figure 16).

All levels of compensation require the instigation of a "compensation and maintenance agreement" identifying the amount and form of compensation to be paid to the property owner subject to agreed works and portions of building that will require continued maintenance in the long term. The maintenance agreement is attached to the title deeds of the property, along with the byelaw. This is an extremely powerful tool because it protects the building from demolition in perpetuity. To ensure that maintenance agreements are adhered to, the City must carry out annual inspections and five-yearly reviews of designated properties for compliance.

The City of Edmonton have estimated that every CD$1 foregone in property tax under their property tax compensation programme is balanced by about CD$14 worth of building work.

Property tax incentives and transfer of development rights, Edmonton, Canada

The municipal property tax rebate (compensation) system offered by the City of Edmonton in Alberta, Canada has acted as an incentive to restore and rehabilitate (rather than demolish) heritage property.

Figure 15 – MacDonald Hotel, Edmonton.

After a number of years of lying empty, this building was restored and rehabilitated, benefiting from a property tax rebate of about CD$900 000 from the municipal authority (by which the property tax was frozen at pre-rehabilitation levels for five years) (Level 3 compensation). The rehabilitation project was provided with financial security through a transfer development right allowing the owners the right to build a 10-storey commercial structure on the park in front of the hotel or to sell this right on the open market.

Figure 16 – Union Bank Inn, Edmonton.

Former bank building rehabilitated as bed and breakfast accommodation with assistance of approximately CD$200 000 to pay for the restoration of architecturally significant features (Level 3 alternative compensation).

5.4.11. Other considerations

If property tax is based on the market value of the land, determined by the development potential of nearby sites, the tax may encourage demolition of historic buildings (in order to obtain a higher value from redevelopment). However, the prevention of demolition can be linked to property tax incentives, as evidenced in Denmark, the USA and Canada (above).

5.4.12. Tax incentives in the purchase price of property

In some countries, there are tax incentives related to the taxes payable on the purchase of protected property. In Spain, expenditure on a property used as a main residence and included in the General Register of Properties of Cultural Interest is given a tax credit equivalent to 15% of such expenditure (capped at €9 015). In Italy, registration fees payable on the market value of purchased property are reduced from 7 to 3% for protected property (subject to the requirement that the owner respects the obligation to conserve the building – a penalty is applied if no action is taken within a two-year period). In the Netherlands, foundations that specialise in restoring historic buildings are exempt from conveyance tax and protected buildings that are open to the public are exempt from wealth tax.

5.5. Value added tax (VAT) or sales tax incentives

A reduced rate of, or exemption from, VAT on the sale of goods (such as building materials) and services (such as the supply of services by conservation operators/building enterprises) could provide significant benefits to the architectural heritage. However, there are very few examples in Europe of VAT relief, despite the fact that this would provide a significant spur to encourage the upkeep of heritage properties. This problem was scrutinised by the Council of Europe in a detailed examination of the issue in 2003, but there has not been significant change since this date. The opportunity to reduce VAT rates specifically for historic buildings is limited by the tax harmonisation policy of the European Union, though some countries apply lower rates of VAT to dwellings, which may benefit protected buildings used as homes. However, it is rare for VAT relief to be given directly to architectural heritage property.

5.5.1. Non-heritage VAT exemptions

In Belgium the VAT rate is 21%, but a lower rate of 6% applies to construction, renovation, rehabilitation, improvement and repair of all dwellings that have been in use for more than 15 years. In France the standard rate of VAT is 20.6%, but a lower rate of 5.5% applies to all dwellings more than two years old. Similar provisions apply in Italy (standard rate 20%, lower rate for dwellings 10%, with no building age limit). For painting and stucco work to dwellings over 20 years old in the Netherlands, a lower rate of 6% applies (where the standard rate of VAT is 17.5%). In Ireland a lower rate of 12.5% applies to general construction activity (standard rate 21%), whether the building is protected or not.

5.5.2. Specific VAT exemptions for heritage buildings

In Spain and the United Kingdom there are specific exemptions from VAT for the protected heritage. In Spain, all work on historic buildings is charged at a lower rate of 7%. In the United Kingdom, materials and services supplied to execute alterations to listed buildings (protected structures) and scheduled ancient monuments are VAT-exempt, provided that any alterations are approved by the relevant authority and that the requisite consents have been obtained. However, the conservation lobby has long regarded this as an anomaly because, though it can encourage rehabilitation (in approved circumstances), nonetheless essential repair and restoration work does not benefit from the exemption. This is an incentive to alter the character of buildings (and a disincentive to undertake proper maintenance), and pressure for change has led to a partial change in the exemption, albeit not for all buildings/structures. From 2001 an interim grant measure covered the difference between VAT at 17.5% and at 5% for listed places of worship. In 2004 this relief on building repairs was extended to cover the full rate of 17.5% until 2006 and this has been further extended until 2010, with additional relief to cover professional fees and repairs to fixtures and fittings.

5.5.3. Sales tax relief in North America

In North America there are a number of examples of sales tax relief (equivalent to VAT). For example, the Canadian Province of Nova Scotia administers a sales tax rebate programme giving a rebate of provincial sales tax on building materials and labour used in the restoration of designated heritage buildings and properties in Heritage Conservation Districts. This represents an acknowledgement by the government of the contribution made by the private property owner to heritage conservation. To ensure that good conservation practice has been adhered to, applicants must provide detailed receipts and supporting documentation for all projects. In the USA, a number of states (such as Kentucky and Texas) provide certain types of sales tax exemption whereby non-profit organisations owning historic properties are exempt from paying sales tax on materials used to rehabilitate or operate eligible property and also from collecting sales tax on admission fees for opening such property to the public.

5.6. Sponsorship and donation incentives

Philanthropy has an important role in funding the preservation of architectural heritage, and it can be supported by tax measures encouraging personal donations and commercial sponsorship. To encourage individuals, income tax relief can be given on sums donated for this purpose and, similarly, businesses can be encouraged in sponsorship activity by relief from company taxes. Charitable and other non-profit organisations and foundations set up to support works to protected structures or to manage such property can benefit from this type of support. Some incentives for sponsoring specifically require that donations are given to a specialist foundation for heritage conservation. These types of organisation have a part to play in funding architectural heritage, particularly when state budgets are constrained (see sections 2.1, Charitable Trusts and 2.2, Heritage Foundations).

These types of incentive can be illustrated by examples from a number of countries.

5.6.1. Belgium

Cash donations between €250 and €500 000 per year to support work (but not day-to-day management) on heritage projects may be deducted from the taxable income of companies or individuals if the recipient is an institution specified by law or by royal decree (for example, restoration projects carried out by the organisation Flanders Heritage). Further relief for business taxpayers can be given for sponsoring heritage projects. Sponsorship costs, such as advertising, are fiscally deductible (subject to certain conditions).

5.6.2. Denmark

Private companies in Denmark can set up foundations to support charitable activities such as heritage conservation. These foundations may top up the funding that an applicant has already been offered in state aid for an approved scheme of works. The fact that a scheme is receiving state funding gives security to the foundation that their funds are being spent on a worthwhile project. The Velux Window Company supports architectural heritage conservation projects in Denmark through such a foundation.

5.6.3. France

Sponsorship policy is well developed in France, whose system is a good exemplar.

In general, companies in France may deduct any unconditional paid sponsorship to projects and bodies of general public interest from their taxable profit. This legislation, dating from 1987, distinguishes between expenditure incurred without consideration (unconditional gifts) and expenditure incurred with consideration (sponsorship), where all cultural heritage expenditure is deductible from taxable profits if it is incurred for the direct benefit of the firm. Deductions are normally subject to an upper limit as a percentage of turnover, but a higher percentage applies where the beneficiaries of sponsorship are public-interest associations or foundations. In the heritage context, the legislation allows firms to deduct from net profits the charges incurred in the purchase, rental and maintenance of stately homes that are classified historic monuments, listed with the title of historic monument or otherwise approved.

Firms wishing to develop their sponsorship policy can do this through several types of foundations that support various public-interest issues, including some that specialise in cultural, environmental and heritage issues (see section 2.2.1).

5.6.4. Germany

Donations towards the conservation and restoration of architectural heritage can be set against income and corporation tax at a rate of 10%. Tax deductions for large donations may be spread over several years. Since 1999, there are higher tax deductions for donations to foundations. For example, Deutsche Stiftung Denkmalschutz, a national foundation for architectural heritage (part-funded by the federal government), raises almost half its funding from private donations (see section 2.2 Heritage Foundations). The foundation supports requests for assistance from monument owners, or where there are social problems and a need for community support, and can assist smaller specific building foundations. Foundations do not pay taxes until a specified level of gain is made, at which point support can be transferred to a limited holding company to work on a non-profit basis on buildings in need of action.

5.6.5. Ireland

In Ireland, individual and corporate taxpayers are entitled to tax deductions for donations of money or property to non-profit eligible charities, including those supporting heritage, such as An Taisce – the National Trust for Ireland, established in 1948. In 2006, the Irish Government established the Irish Heritage Trust, a charitable body, with a mandate to acquire property of significant heritage value. The government set up an endowment fund and provided for tax deductions for cash donations from private and corporate sponsors (subject to a ceiling of €6 million). An owner who transfers ownership of heritage property to the Irish Heritage Trust may remain living in the property for their lifetime as well as receiving tax incentives.

5.6.6. Italy

Individual taxpayers can donate 0.8% of their annual tax liability to the Minister of Cultural Assets to help fund programmes for the restoration of important monuments.

5.6.7. Netherlands

Cash donations and the transfer of property to non-profit heritage foundations and non-profit public housing corporations entitle individual and corporate donors to tax exemptions. Heritage trusts and foundations in turn fund heritage conservation work, such as the purchase, restoration and maintenance of historic property, and the provision of social housing.

5.6.8. Spain

Individual and corporate donations to appropriate entities for the benefit of Spanish historical heritage assets entitle donors to a tax deduction of 20%. Beneficiary entities include national heritage foundations, the state, autonomous regions, local corporations and the Church. Some autonomous regions have established their own tax deduction mechanism for heritage protection. For example, the Region of Murcia offers economic donation deductions for heritage preservation action in the region.

5.6.9. United Kingdom

Encouragement of philanthropy and private patronage of charitable organisations set up to support culture (including heritage) has been given through a simplified tax regime introduced by the UK Government. Since 2000, gifts of cash by individuals of any amount (subject to the limit of total tax liability) have been eligible for income tax relief and individuals may also gift quoted shares without any tax liability on the value of the shares and with full income tax relief. Donations of cash by companies can also be set against accounts for tax purposes.

In the heritage context, there are a number of charitable organisations that may benefit from such charitable donations. The Architectural Heritage Fund is a registered charity founded in 1976 to promote the conservation of historic buildings in the UK by providing advice, information and financial assistance in the form of grants and low-interest working capital loans for projects undertaken by building preservation trusts, which are usually registered as charitable organisations and act in a non-profit manner to repair and rehabilitate historic buildings, and other charities. The National Trust (National Trust, 1895 for the UK; National Trust for Scotland, 1931) is a registered charity that owns and manages a large number of heritage properties and relies on financial support from members' subscriptions (over three million members of the National Trust and 270 000 members of the National Trust for Scotland) as well as gifts, legacies and volunteer activity. (See section 2.1, Charitable Trusts.)

5.6.10. USA

Cash donations and transfers of property to a registered non-profit charitable heritage trust or foundation entitle donors to tax deductions. The level of deduction varies from state to state.

In some states, businesses are encouraged by enabling legislation to own, use and rehabilitate historic properties, aided by specific tax credits and exemptions. Businesses with offices in historic industrial mills in Rhode Island can claim a business tax credit for interest earned and paid on loans made for eligible business expenses or costs incurred in rehabilitating the mill and against salaries paid to employees working in the mill. In Maryland, financial institutions and public service companies can claim a franchise tax credit for undertaking rehabilitation of a certified historic property. Corporations in Florida receive a community contribution tax credit for donations to approved historic preservation projects. Public corporations in Washington DC are exempt from an annual excise tax for certified historic structures. A prominent example of corporate sponsorship is the Disney Corporation's redevelopment of Times Square in New York, which included renovation of a landmark theatre.

5.6.11. Canada

Canada has a variety of heritage organisations, foundations and non-profit bodies registered as charitable trusts, which give charitable tax receipts for donations so that donors can reclaim income tax on the amount given. Examples include, at federal level, the Heritage Canada Foundation, created by the federal government as a non-governmental charity in 1973, and at provincial level various similar charitable trust heritage organisations, such as the Ontario Heritage Foundation (see sections 2.1.3 and 2.1.4).

5.7. Transfer, inheritance and capital gains tax incentives

Incentives from these tax mechanisms help to prevent the dismantling of private properties, which often occurs on change of ownership, resulting in a failure to maintain the monument, its abandonment or its repurchase by a local authority, thus adding to the burden of public expenditure on the heritage. A number of countries offer such incentives.

5.7.1. Belgium

Transfer of a classified monument in the Brussels-Capital region to the regional authority or a foundation with the legal status of an established public utility is exempt from inheritance and gift tax.

5.7.2. France

Classified monuments and those in the supplementary inventory are fully exempt from inheritance and capital transfer tax, though this exemption is effective only where a standard agreement has been concluded between the state and the beneficiaries. In order to qualify, the owner must sign an agreement of indefinite duration with the state, giving various undertakings (such as opening the monument to the public, maintaining it, retaining and displaying integral fixtures and fittings, and making the property available free of charge for local community events). If the conditions of the agreement cease to apply, capital transfer tax must be paid. Classified monuments held by family-run property companies constituted under civil law are also exempt from inheritance and capital transfer duties.

5.7.3. Germany

Architectural monuments are exempt or partially exempt from inheritance tax (and gift tax) as long as conservation of the asset is in the public interest and the income generated from the property is lower than the expenses incurred. Inheritance tax may be levied if the conditions giving rise to the exemption cease to apply (or the property is resold) within 10 years. This provides a strong incentive to retain property in private ownership with family continuity.

Full exemption is given to owners who voluntarily decide to open their building to the public and opt to make the building subject to the relevant legislation on heritage conservation, as long as the building has been protected or owned by the same family for at least 20 years. Partial exemption (of 60%) is granted if the owner allows access (as far as is possible) to researchers or the public. The inheritance tax base may also be reduced to take account of the constraints imposed on an owner in relation to a protected building.

5.7.4. Ireland

Exemption from inheritance and gift taxes is allowed for historic buildings that have been approved by the relevant tax authority, so long as reasonable public access is made available and the property is retained by the successor for at least six years.

5.7.5. Italy

A capital gain realised on the sale of a protected building was taxable, but at 75% of the rate applied to non-protected buildings. However, since 1 January 2003 no capital gains tax is payable on any property.

Protected buildings are exempt from inheritance tax; however, this tax advantage is removed if the property is sold within five years of the succession or if the heir fails to comply with legislative requirements on protected properties. Preferential tax treatment is also given for gifted protected property, which is subject to a flat-rate tax set at €130 (the gift tax on other property is set at 3 to 7% of the property's value).

5.7.6. Netherlands

A gift or bequest to a certified social or cultural organisation of a protected monument (historic building) that is open to the public is exempt from inheritance and gift tax.

5.7.7. Spain

All properties that qualify as "properties of cultural interest" under national law (or are protected under the law of an autonomous region) are given an allowance equivalent to 95% of the value when assessing estate duties for inheritance tax, subject to the requirement that the heir is the spouse or a descendant; the tax benefit is rescinded if the heir sells the property within 10 years. In some autonomous regions, such as Catalonia, all heirs are granted the allowance for properties protected under regional law.

Properties transferred by way of a lifetime gift to a spouse or descendant are also given the 95% allowance, provided that the donor is at least 65 years old at the time of the gift and the beneficiary keeps the property for at least 10 years.

5.7.8. United Kingdom

An exemption from inheritance tax is given for a limited category of buildings of outstanding historic or architectural interest (for example, stately homes or large country houses) when they pass to a new owner. The property, which includes the house and any land that forms an essential part of its character (such as a designed park or landscape) must be certified as meeting the criteria. The new owner is required to give reasonable public access and to undertake to maintain the building and grounds. Owners of approved buildings of outstanding historic or architectural interest may establish a heritage maintenance fund for this purpose. Property transferred into these funds is exempt from capital gains tax and inheritance tax.

The practice of transferring the ownership of property to the National Trust (see section 2.1.1), particularly in the case of country houses, not only allows the owner to retain certain residency rights but has proved invaluable for the maintenance of such buildings. This approach has also been adopted by the Pro Patrimonio Foundation, based in Romania.

5.7.9. USA

Donors are entitled to charitable contribution deductions from federal estate tax (a form of inheritance tax) for the donation of a full or partial conservation easement (see section 2.5) in relation to historic property to a qualified organisation such as a registered non-profit charitable heritage trust or foundation, or a government entity. Federal gift tax or capital gains tax payable on property given or sold after it is placed under easement may also be reduced because of the property's resulting reduced value.

5.7.10. Canada

There is no inheritance tax in Canada and there are few donations of heritage property, largely because the federal government collects capital gains tax on donated real property. Since 1998 donors can deduct from their net income 75% of the value of a heritage property donated to the national government or a charity; previously the limit was more stringent. Similarly, national tax policies do not permit deductions for donations made as part of heritage conservation easements (see section 2.5). There has been a campaign to amend the Income Tax Act to end capital gains tax on donations of heritage sites to charities. This would make it attractive for an owner to donate a historic place to charity rather than demolish it.

6. Integrated heritage funding strategies: administration and management

6.0. Introduction

The Council of Europe's Recommendation No. R (91) 6, on measures likely to support funding of the conservation of architectural heritage, identified the need for favourable conditions for the initiation of projects. The administrative measures recommended included the adoption of appropriate urban development strategies, drawing the attention of potential investors to sources of funding and opportunities for rehabilitating architectural heritage, appropriate forms of management plans for areas, simplified procedures and efficient forms of project co-ordination, including partnerships between public and private sectors.

Integrated heritage funding systems can also be directed at improving social conditions, by providing social housing in rehabilitated buildings, to be let at affordable rents for people on low incomes, and by recognising that the built heritage can make a contribution to quality of life. Area-based integrated strategies for older areas will also need to consider development needs, such as infrastructure, traffic planning, housing, commerce and tourism. Addressing these wider issues so that heritage can be a factor or catalyst in sustainable economic and social development will require the combining of finance from the state, local authorities, public bodies and the private sector, along with integrated pro-active instruments (national and regional spatial plans, urban land-use plans and specific action plan mechanisms).

Some of these issues have already been examined in chapters 3 and 5 above. For example:

• In Denmark, housing improvement and urban renewal programmes (section 3.3.1) are often led and managed by private-sector companies specialising in urban renewal. State funding to local authorities can be redirected for this purpose. Such companies can direct renewal of older areas and conversion of buildings in municipal ownership so as to meet social housing needs, with the finished scheme being sold to a social housing corporation, the aim being to avoid gentrification and maintain existing communities. By this means, tenants receiving social welfare benefits are entitled to rent subsidies. Furthermore, urban renewal schemes for housing can be linked to a municipal preservation plan ("preservation atlas") to assist external improvements on buildings "worthy of preservation" (not listed).

- In England, area-based, heritage-led regeneration funding (section 3.3.3) has concentrated action on historic areas with social and economic problems. The heritage funding mechanisms are linked to management plans for areas (such as "action area plans") and specific heritage funding programmes, but additional regeneration funding may be provided through partnerships between different agencies.

- In France (section 3.3.4), housing improvement areas (OPAH) with a heritage component support architectural reinstatement. The national housing agency (ANAH) can subsidise work on historic properties to let to low-income families as part of the renovation scheme. In a protected zone (ZZAUP), the emphasis is on rehabilitation and economic and social regeneration, offering aid to improve façades and public spaces, and tax incentives for landlords who restore residential properties for rent (for a minimum period).

- In Germany (section 3.3.5), the *Städtebaulicher Denkmalschutz* programme of urban renewal in historic inner areas, for example, included improving the quality of housing. The towns and cities in eastern Germany that benefited from this programme have seen an increase in the number of inhabitants of about 40% and a resulting revived sense of community. In small towns in particular, the traditional mixed social structure has been strengthened by low-income inhabitants who have moved because of rent rises elsewhere and high-income inhabitants choosing to move there. Furthermore, the programme was recognised to have considerable advantages over normal state heritage-aid programmes as it tackled problems in a comprehensive manner (dealing with protected buildings and groups of buildings, the context of monuments, streets, environment, service infrastructure and so on) and also drew on other existing funding. The focus was on sustainable development of historic inner cities, socially-orientated holistic and integrated urban renewal, and urban development that preserved heritage resources in over 100 towns.

- In the USA, in addition to the rehabilitation tax credit, a tax credit has been provided for converting historic buildings to low-income housing (section 5.3.1). It has been found that such schemes benefit

historic-building owners and developers, gaining community accept-
ance for affordable housing schemes that rehabilitate historic buildings. They benefit tenants, who are able to enjoy the amenities of
living in historic spaces (with historic detailing), which can serve a
social function as common spaces where tenants can meet. The
community also benefits, because the rehabilitation of buildings
provides continuity and stability – people identify with the retention
of existing buildings.

6.1. Partnerships and management structures

Funding partnerships – combining different levels of government
(state, regional and local) with other stakeholders like non-governmental organisations, non-profit bodies, corporate entities and other
parts of the private sector – allow the risks and returns of architectural
heritage conservation strategies to be shared. The diversity offered
by the many possible partnership structures, from high-budget to a
simple exchange of information and expertise, allows a wide range of
resources and skills to be brought together.

The creation of partnerships has become a common mechanism for
co-ordinating activities in area-based, heritage-led funding strategies.
The scene of collaborative effort may be a historic centre or quarter,
or a rural area with significant heritage interest that has suffered
economic, social and physical problems. Partnerships can involve
bodies with broad, often disparate interests in the historical, cultural,
social, economic and physical character of the defined area. Through
this approach, issues can be tackled in a comprehensive and holistic
manner, making use of funding for housing improvement, the provision of business premises, training, employment and infrastructure, as
well as specific heritage funding for the built fabric.

The establishment of a partnership between funding organisations
and stakeholders, all very different, within a heritage-led regeneration/
rehabilitation project can sometimes be complex. Compromises may
need to be made to achieve a balance of power and satisfy the diver-
gent objectives of stakeholders. Specific planning instruments, such as
preservation, enhancement or action plans, may assist in developing
a coherent and transparent strategy; a suitable management board
or agency may need to be set up that reflects the partnership agreement between different levels of government, public funding agencies, community representatives (including residents and businesses)

and non-profit organisations; a system will be needed to control development, preservation and enhancement action, stimulate investment and guide conservation and rehabilitation, and it will need a suitable administrative structure.

The Parliamentary Assembly of the Council of Europe has given weight to the idea of developing appropriate public–private partnerships for the management of cultural property in Recommendation 1730 (2005) The private management of cultural property, adopted by the Standing Committee acting on behalf of the Assembly on 25 November 2005, and a Report of the Committee on Culture, Science and Education with the same title (Doc. 10731, 24 October 2005) debated by the Standing Committee.

6.2. Examples of specific management organisations and partnerships

Suitable management structures and agencies working to co-ordinate activities can be seen in the following examples from different countries, including specific case studies.

6.2.1. Germany

The legal structure of an area heritage funding programme in Germany (see section 3.3.5) requires the municipality to set up a management bureau (project office or *Sanierungstrager*) to provide information, advice and support to monument owners, to promote and explain the grant aid possibilities from different sources and to assist the completion of grant applications. This bureau can be set up by the municipal building authority or by a well-established architectural company acting as agent for the municipality. Often a local company is used, such as a company of architects and town planners. Local companies tend to be more informed about legal and financial matters such as potential sources of funding from small foundations working in the area, and close proximity to the project is good for maintaining contact with owners and overseeing work in progress. The relevant state authority for cultural heritage covers the cost of providing the management bureau.

The bureau or agency usually performs the task of managing the area revitalisation strategy on behalf of the local authority, under its supervision. It will organise a plan of works each year, dealing with individual buildings, infrastructure, roads and underground works (which must be co-ordinated with water, electricity and telephone authorities). Often municipal authorities do not have sufficient knowledge of conservation, so a specialist private company running the project office can advise the authority and persuade building owners to take suitable action.

The management bureau informs owners how they might combine financial assistance from various aid programmes, which may include specific heritage funding, town renewal schemes and more general modernisation programmes to update the services of older properties. The project office may also be used to administer funds as the municipality's trustee.

Many towns in eastern Germany were supported after reunification by the *Städtbaulicher Denkmalschutz* funding programme (1991-97), which tackled problems in a comprehensive manner by dealing with protected buildings and groups of buildings, the context of monuments, streets, environment, service infrastructure and so on, and drawing on existing funding. In towns such as Weimar and Erfurt a project office (sometimes more than one) was established to co-ordinate these actions. In the old quarter of Erfurt two agencies were set up, and a further agency was established to co-ordinate action in an adjoining area.

6.2.2. Spain

An example of a management structure to co-ordinate action and finance can be found in the historic city of Santiago de Compostela.

i. Example: Santiago de Compostela

In 1997 the special plan for protection and rehabilitation of the historic city was approved, with the aim of assisting the protection of architectural heritage and improving business, institutional and residential facilities through building rehabilitation, new development and environmental improvements.

A special heritage body, Real Patronato de la Ciudad de Santiago, was set up for the purpose of conserving, restoring and rehabilitating the city's heritage under the patronage of the King of Spain, with representatives of the three levels of government (local, regional and national), as well as the university and the Church. From this an executive body was set up, the City Consortium, chaired by the mayor and comprising representatives of each level of government with the aim of taking decisions by consensus. On the budgetary front, the state contributed 60%, the regional authority 35% and the municipality 5% of overall funding. The basic aim of the consortium was to channel various actions into one overall strategy that all three levels of government would implement on an annual basis. The scheme covered major investment, normally earmarked for development areas outside the city walls, and operations inside the historic centre.

Among its initiatives, the City Consortium established a subordinate Rehabilitation Office staffed by professionals from different disciplines. This office co-ordinated various actions:

- analysis of the condition of historic buildings;
- analysis of social and economic problems in the area;
- awareness-raising of the benefits of rehabilitation (jointly with the local authority);
- technical and administrative support, including a "one-stop shop" (technicians brought together from various competent departments) to enable owners and residents to overcome obstacles like the issue of permits, or to inform them on finance, qualified building enterprises and other germane questions;
- lightweight intervention, with rehabilitation following guidelines in the special plan;
- implementation of specific financial support in three phases: housing improvement, improvement of commercial premises, restoration/ conservation of specific buildings (such as theatres, markets and churches).

In the two years following the approval of the special plan, rehabilitation action culminated in completed projects involving 323 dwellings, 435 commercial premises and 8 hotels.

6.2.3. France

In France the focus of conservation has gradually progressed from individual monuments to urban areas and landscapes. From the 1960s this trend led to a more comprehensive approach entailing the protection of entire sites, groups of buildings and public areas, delimited by legal instruments. One of the main tools of area-based mechanisms is the designation of *secteurs sauvegardés* (conservation areas) under the provisions of a *plan de sauvegarde et de mise en valeur* (PSMV: preservation and enhancement plan).

This procedure mainly concerns towns and cities with historic centres, sometimes showing a decline in their population, characterised by a high concentration of old buildings (see Figures 10 and 11). Decentralisation laws in the 1980s and 1990s transferred responsibility for town planning to local and regional authorities, which led to the introduction of contractual instruments for heritage conservation and management. The state and the local authorities agree to define *zones de protection du patrimoine architectural, urbain et paysager* (ZPPAUPs: architectural, urban and landscape heritage protection zones), whose purpose is to protect and manage the urban and rural heritage, of built areas and landscapes, on a contractual basis, allocating responsibilities between central government and local authorities.

However, housing improvement programmes (OPAH) also have a role to play in the context of organising action in older residential quarters.

i. Example: Belleville OPAH (Paris)

An OPAH programme was set up in Belleville, an older housing district of Paris, in 1998. As with other OPAH schemes, a private project office (or *pacte*) was selected by the municipality to run the scheme (in this case, the Pacte de Paris). The project team comprised a variety of professional expertise – architecture, urban planning, project management and housing – as well as technical and secretarial staff. The project office, in the heart of the district, acted as an information office for the OPAH and co-ordination bureau for the scheme, giving advice on works to rented or owner-occupied property, undertaking research and co-ordinating applications for financial aid from state, regional and municipal sources.

The Belleville district was originally designated as a comprehensive development zone by the Paris municipality – authorising state intervention to undertake or commission the demolition and redevelopment of the area. However, as a result of resistance by residents and landlords in Belleville, this was abandoned in 1995. Belleville OPAH began in 1998, incorporating financial incentives for both owner-occupiers and landlords, with a life span of six years.

The project was developed by the Pacte de Paris on the basis that cleared sites in public ownership within the OPAH boundary should be redeveloped for social housing and existing buildings could be improved. There were at least 86 properties within the OPAH boundary containing a total of 2 330 rented apartments, most of which were in need of improvement (see Figure 17). The Belleville OPAH boundary coincided with a state-designated area in which the municipality and the state would work to improve social and economic conditions.

The five objectives of the OPAH programme in Belleville run by the Pacte de Paris were:

- to improve living conditions by new heating, water, sanitation and electrical services;
- to improve energy conservation, particularly through double glazing and insulation;
- to resolve problems of unsanitary and unhealthy conditions in buildings, including the health hazard from lead in paint;
- to encourage lower rents with the renovation lease mechanism whereby ANAH (the national housing agency) gave financial help to landlords for improving their property (if the owner agreed to let apartments at low rents for at least 10 years and not to sell or live in the apartments during that period);
- to make architectural improvements: reinstating windows and other façade features, work on staircases, providing fire escapes, improving basements and creating larger apartments by amalgamating smaller units (see Figure 18).

The Pacte de Paris co-ordinated subsidies for landlords (from ANAH and the municipality) to improve housing standards, including sanitation works, with varying levels of financial aid depending on the level of rent to be achieved. About 70% of the apartment buildings in Belleville were co-owned by groups of up to 20 people and run by independent estate managers (syndicates) regulated by co-ownership legislation. If a landlord made alterations to an old building that did not respect architectural detail, the Pacte de Paris was able to enforce appropriate changes and withhold financial aid until the work had been done more sensitively.

The Pacte de Paris also co-ordinated subsidies for owner-occupiers, who would not normally be entitled to grants through OPAH programmes (ANAH supports work on rented residential property only), but here the state, region and municipality provided financial assistance to owner-occupiers based on a means test. The standard home-improvement grant in Belleville was 25 or 30% (depending on the owner's taxable income) of the cost of work to apartments and common areas, with a maximum limit of €10 671. The state inspector (Prefecture) identified 13 co-owned buildings in Belleville as having particular problems. As a result, these received higher grants of 30 or 40% (depending on taxable income) of the cost of works in common areas like stairs, corridors, roofs and façades, with a maximum limit of €12 958. If the suggested works fulfilled the five stated objectives of the OPAH, they were given priority status and could receive an extra 20% grant from the municipality. If they were not a priority, the municipality would give only 10% extra grant. If the landlord would not carry out necessary work to a residential building, the tenant could apply to the Pacte de Paris management office for grant aid to carry out the work once consent was obtained from the landlord.

Building owners issued with a notice by the state inspector to carry out immediate works (usually with two months' notice) to resolve unsanitary conditions could apply for additional grants to cover 50% of the cost of works to common parts and apartments, subject to a maximum limit and a requirement to complete the works within the specified time limit (or otherwise the state had powers to intervene to carry out the necessary works and enforce payment of costs from the owner). The Centre of Social Action in Paris gave further help to residents on low incomes.

If necessary, the Pacte de Paris could also organise low-interest loans (at 1%) within the OPAH (through specific social funds). Where beneficiaries of financial assistance experienced cash-flow problems, the municipality could offer pre-financing. Funds were also available to cover necessary works where owners were found to be in debt.

Development speculation following the introduction of public funding through OPAHs has been known to attract unscrupulous developers (increasing the incidence of sub-standard work and further sub-division of buildings, increasing co-ownership difficulties). To avoid this situation, the municipality gave vendors the option to sell their property to a private housing association, of which there are about 10 in Paris. The local foundation in Belleville, La Fondation Habitier, is restricted to the creation of social housing and is tax-exempt due to its status as a non-profit organisation.

Other OPAHs have been set up in historic towns with buildings of heritage quality, such as Rochefort, where an OPAH was one part of a managed rehabilitation strategy.

Belleville Operations Programmées d'Amélioration de l'Habitat, (OPAH) (planned housing improvement operations), Paris, France

Figure 17 – Buildings in poor condition on the corner of rue Dénoyez and rue Ramponeau. All the properties on these two roads were identified for action via the Belleville OPAH.

Figure 18 – Rehabilitated housing in rue Lesage within the Belleville OPAH including the reinstatement of architectural façade features.

ii. Example: Rochefort rehabilitation strategy

The renewal of the historic naval town of Rochefort began in the 1970s when a political group calling itself Rochefort's Renaissance took advantage of a procedure known as *contrat ville moyenne* – a state funding initiative to enhance the status of small towns. Preliminary studies assisted by a town planning institute identified that rehabilitation and re-use of the built heritage was preferable to new construction and this guided urban development policy for the next 20 years. A flagship project was developed to rehabilitate the Corderie Royale (a former ropeworks building) for new uses including a municipal library, a media centre, a chamber for commerce and industry, and other uses, and to create a public park around it.

Following completion of the project in 1988, a new initiative was launched, starting with an analysis of the urban heritage (the town had a remarkably homogeneous ancient centre) and formulation of an architectural charter for the town, which identified features that should be preserved. Heritage workshops were used to raise the inhabitants' awareness of the town's qualities.

Local politicians set up a special town-planning service as the management structure, with broad powers to draft a land-use plan, manage major rehabilitation projects, deal with building permits and provide institutional communication. This service had a small interdisciplinary team (including architects and town planners) motivated to restoring the past grandeur of the town, which sought finance for each project from *département*, regional and state authorities as well as from European funds.

An essential part of the revitalisation was the establishment of a series of OPAH schemes (between 1991 and 1998) to rehabilitate older houses, including a pilot scheme in 1996-98 to rehabilitate vacant dwellings above shops that had been left empty or used as stores (similar to the LOTS approach used in the United Kingdom: see section 6.2.4). ANAH gave financial support to owners of rented property (the "renovation lease" approach) and other state sources aided housing improvement for owner-occupiers. Low-interest loans were also provided by the state to support rehabilitation action.

These actions to revitalise this historic town were successful due to the decompartmentalised nature of the special municipal management structure, which acted collectively on each issue, rather than the specialists in building, infrastructure, protection and the rest remaining apart.

6.2.4. United Kingdom

Area-based funding mechanisms for heritage-led regeneration schemes in the UK usually work on a partnership basis (between different public authorities and funding agencies and the private sector) and therefore require a management structure.

The Grainger Town Project provides a good exemplar in this respect. It has been seen as a demonstration of best practice, gaining national and international recognition through the winning of various prestigious awards:

- 2002: Best Practice Award from the British Urban Regeneration Association;
- 2002: Commendation for planning achievement by the Royal Town Planning Institute;
- 2002: Buildings short-listed for a conservation award by the Royal Institute of Chartered Surveyors;
- 2003: Winner of the European Union Prize for Culture Heritage and the Europa Nostra Award in recognition of "its use of culture to breathe new life into the city landscape";
- 2003: Best Completed Project Award from the Association of Town Centre Management;
- 2004: Royal Town Planning Institute Award, the Silver Cup.

Moreover, following a conference entitled "Investing in the heritage" hosted by the Grainger Town Partnership in 2002, a European network – INHERIT – was set up, based around the concept of investing in heritage to regenerate Europe's historic cities. This network was formed during the last year of the Grainger Town project by the partnership in conjunction with the city council and the European Association of Historic Towns and Regions (EAHTR). In 2007 it published a good-practice guide to successful heritage-led regeneration and reported on EU regional policies and funding mechanisms relating to cultural heritage and regeneration.

i. Example: Grainger Town, Newcastle upon Tyne

Grainger Town, the name given to the historic core of this city, has one of the highest densities of protected listed buildings in England (40% of the 500 or so buildings in the area) and a higher-than-average number of grade I and II* listed buildings (30% compared to the national average of 6%). In 1992 Newcastle City Council, English Heritage (the government's statutory adviser on the historic environment) and the government Department of the Environment jointly commissioned a study of the area. It was found that it suffered from a lack of economic confidence, under-use of buildings, fabric decay and other environmental problems, including congestion and erosion caused by road traffic. The study set out a conservation-based strategy, which was essentially a planning framework for the area, though it did propose a regeneration strategy that could be developed in partnership with the private sector.

In a subsequent detailed survey of the condition and vacancy of buildings in the area it was found that there was a high number of listed buildings at risk (244) from disrepair or vacancy (47% against the national average of 7%) and many more in a marginal condition and vulnerable to becoming at risk (29% against the national average of 14%) (see Figures 19 and 20).

A Conservation Areas Partnership Scheme (CAPS) was established in Grainger Town in 1994, covering 36 hectares of the city centre (see section 3.3.3 [ii]); this was one of 15 pilot CAPS partnership funding schemes in the country, operated jointly by local councils and English Heritage. The creation of CAPS ensured that the area's conservation budget rose to nearly £500 000 per annum (whereas previously the conservation budget for the whole city had been just £60 000 per annum). In the same year, a small three-year Single Regeneration Budget (SRB) funding scheme was begun by English Partnerships (a national regeneration agency), which provided grant aid for converting the upper floors of listed properties for residential use – known as Living Over The Shop or LOTS (see Figure 21).

As time went on, the area suffered further problems despite some successes in rehabilitating buildings, with grant aid being offered for up to 80% of costs. The number of people in employment in the Grainger Town area fell by nearly 5 000 between 1992 and 1997, and there was a decrease in businesses and residents in the area. The city council and English Heritage, along with English Partnerships, agreed that the area could no longer be left to take care of itself and was in need of a comprehensive regeneration strategy, but one that would secure the past (the heritage qualities of the area) while securing its long-term future (in other words a sustainable approach).

In 1996 consultants EDAW were commissioned to produce a regeneration strategy for Grainger Town and to prepare a bid for government funding. A detailed analysis of the area's problems was immediately undertaken. Grainger Town was a complex urban system, which would have to be tackled in a holistic way. EDAW produced a vision statement to reflect the aspirations for Grainger Town in 2006 – it was to become a dynamic and competitive place with a high-quality environment, a place that would play a major role in the regional economy, a distinctive place, and a safe and attractive place to work, live and visit.

The project was developed though a six-year regeneration scheme (1997-2003), which aimed to secure £120 million in regeneration funding from the public and private sectors (at a ratio of 1:2). The core funding – originally estimated to be £40 million from the public sector – came from five separate agencies, two of which supplied funds specifically for conservation, while the others provided general regeneration funds, some of which were incidentally used for conservation purposes in a more general improvement context. The actual public funding achieved by the end of the project in 2003 came notably from:

- Newcastle City Council – funding of £3.2 million used for joint grants with English Heritage of 60 to 80% to private owners or occupiers of decayed historic or vacant buildings to repair them and to improve shop-fronts to a traditional appearance (see Figure 22), and for the secondment of staff to the project delivery team; and
- English Heritage – funding of £940 000 for the repair of historic buildings and shop-fronts through the CAPS scheme and a subsequent Heritage Economic Regeneration Scheme (see section 3.3.3).

This joint grant aid scheme proved to be the catalyst for much more public and private investment from a wide range of agencies.

- Tyneside Training and Enterprise Council (later the Learning and Skills Council), one of a network of Training and Enterprise Councils set up in disadvantaged areas to develop vocational training initiatives and encourage local business enterprise, whose funding helped to bring new life to the area, in particular, by assisting the generation and development of new uses in vacant upper floors of historic buildings.
- English Partnerships (the national regeneration agency, which was afterwards divided into regional development agencies, one of which – ONE North East – became a funding partner) – contributing £25 million, over half of the Project's public funds, which was mainly

used to help private owners to refurbish their upper floors for new residential or office uses.
- The Single Regeneration Budget (SRB) – following the LOTS scheme (see above) – responded to two further bids for funding with a total of £11 million in support of a wide range of regeneration activities, including economic development, infrastructure, improving the environment (such as pedestrianisation schemes to improve the public realm), and training and employment initiatives.

There were also other supporting funds from public sources:
- Heritage Lottery Fund – funding of about £100 000 to support the repair of Grey's Monument, a landmark structure.
- European funding – over £1.8 million from the European Regional Development Fund (for business development, job creation and cultural developments) and the European Social Fund (for training and Youth Enterprise developments), plus a grant of up to £600 000 to restore and rehabilitate an important 18th-century building as offices.

The investment sought to strengthen and develop Grainger Town as a mixed-use, historic urban quarter based on seven inter-related regeneration themes:
- Business Development and Enterprise – to encourage development of existing companies, generate new entrepreneurial activity and broaden the area's economic base;
- Commercial Development – to secure investment and economic activity in a range of uses, including office, retail, leisure and culture, leading to the repair and re-use of historic buildings and the redevelopment of key sites;
- Access to Opportunity – to improve training and employment opportunities for the long-term unemployed in adjoining inner city wards;
- Housing – to increase the residential population by providing a wide range of affordable housing for rent and sale;
- Quality of Environment – to improve the environment and public spaces to enhance Grainger Town's competitiveness as a place to work, live and visit;
- Arts, Culture and Tourism – to promote Grainger Town as a centre for arts, culture and tourism;
- Management, Marketing and Promotion – to improve the overall management and marketing of the area.

Although conservation was not directly mentioned as an activity, the area's high heritage value and the fact that the project was originally conceived in an attempt to conserve Grainger Town, the practice of conservation was deemed to be relevant to each of the seven regeneration themes.

A company limited by guarantee (see section 2.3) was set up to manage and deliver the regeneration programme: the Grainger Town Partnership. This had a board of 20 directors from the public sector (local authority: 6; other public agencies: 6), private sector (6) and community sector (local residents: 2) and was a partnership of equals with no single body in overall control. The board was supported by a Business Forum and a Residents' Forum, as well as specialist advisory panels such as Urban Design and Public Arts panels. The project was implemented by its own Project Delivery Team of 14 officers, based within the area (some of the staff were seconded from the city council's planning and conservation team).

By the end of the project (2003), the forecast private-sector investment of £80 million had been substantially exceeded (£145 million). Other benefits of the project were subsequently recorded in March 2006. Altogether, 121 buildings of historical importance had been improved and brought back into use, 51 more than the target set by the government. Over 80 000 sq. m of floor space had been developed or provided through the rehabilitation of buildings. A number of initiatives helped create 329 new businesses, well above the target of 199. In relation to commercial property, the project had an overall positive effect on the office, retail and leisure property sectors, enabling a large proportion of vacant sites and buildings of historical importance to be brought back into use, thus significantly aiding the conservation-led regeneration of the area. The partnership recorded the creation of 2 299 jobs, against a target of 1 900. A significant amount of work had been created for local workers in construction, and new training opportunities had increased local skills. The residential population had been increased by the provision of 572 new dwelling units (including both affordable housing for rent and other housing for sale) against a target of 522. Improvement and enhancement of the environment had helped to increase developer, investor and consumer confidence in the area. Public art installations and cultural events/festivals had enhanced public spaces and helped to promote the revitalisation of Grainger Town. Marketing and promotion had increased the public's awareness of the value of the area's built heritage.

Linking heritage with regeneration in the Grainger Town Project Heritage Economic Regeneration Scheme, Newcastle upon Tyne, United Kingdom

Figure 19 – Nos. 2-12 Grey Street

A building categorised as being "at risk" which had remained vacant and in disrepair for over 20 years before being rehabilitated.

Figure 20 – Nos. 2-12 Grey Street after being rehabilitated as a hotel

Figure 21 – LOTS (living over the shop)

Grant aid was provided by the government's regeneration agency, English Partnerships, to convert vacant upper floors into residential use.

Figure 22 – The return of traditional shop fronts

Grant aid from English Heritage and the city council helped to fund this work, following standards set out in design guidance.

7. Overview

The aim of this publication has been to produce a comprehensive guide to different measures that may be used to support the funding of architectural heritage. Research for this study was carried out between 1998 and 2008; the information presented has come from a variety of published sources (see Reference Sources) and a range of specialists (see Acknowledgments). However, as laws and tax provisions change over time, there is no guarantee that all the information presented remains current, and inevitably it will be superseded. Nevertheless, the main purpose has been to provide evidence of worthwhile mechanisms in operation.

In Chapter 1 it was indicated that this publication would aim to build upon previous work by the Council of Europe, with particular reference to administrative, intervention and financial measures, as well as specific measures to promote sponsorship, which had been identified in 1991 (sections 1.4 and 1.5).

In relation to administrative measures, Chapter 6 refers to a number of examples of strategies for putting the heritage to use by means of area-based heritage regeneration/rehabilitation projects, including the role of project offices in co-ordinating such action, which may involve different partners. Management boards, whether operated through municipal offices or private or non-profit agencies, have an important role in undertaking studies (analysis of the urban heritage) and identifying action goals, as well as co-ordinating partnership stakeholders and different funding opportunities.

Examples of simplified procedures have been identified in the rehabilitation strategies utilised in Santiago de Compostela (using lightweight intervention following guidelines adopted in a special plan) and Rochefort (with a decompartmentalised special municipal planning service).

Different examples have been presented to show how, by combining funding sources, a more integrated approach can be taken. Moreover, an integrated process can use the heritage as a catalyst for social and economic regeneration of areas, whereby other issues are considered: improvement of the environment and infrastructure, and provision of a range of housing types including social housing and opportunities for business to use rehabilitated heritage property.

Administrative measures for the provision of grant aid and the conditions applied to it, with the use of conservation/management plans, feasibility studies and preliminary works, have been identified in Chapter 3. Although grant-aid programmes can be quite bureaucratic, they can act as a catalyst to private-sector investment in heritage. Such programmes may be more efficient if they are decentralised to local authority level, where they can be directed to areas and buildings most in need (as is the case in the Netherlands and for area-based funding mechanisms in England, for example).

A number of different intervention measures have been identified. Examples of revolving funds, foundations, trusts and limited liability companies managed by private, public, non-governmental organisations and non-profit bodies have been represented by systems operating in different countries. Non-governmental organisations have a significant role to play in promoting conservation and rehabilitation activities and in providing financial support. Large specialised funds and foundations such as the Architectural Heritage Fund and the Deutsche Stiftung Denkmalschutz play an important role in supporting smaller revolving funds and trusts. Such third-sphere bodies are able to operate largely because of the fiscal relief that the non-profit nature of their work (preserving cultural heritage in the public interest) attracts.

Linking housing improvement to the heritage, especially the provision of social housing through the rehabilitation of older buildings, is an important integrated intervention tool. Many such examples have been provided, including the OPAH scheme operated in France and the combining of rehabilitation tax credits with affordable housing tax credits in the USA. A rental policy to support the renovation of buildings for residential use is another important intervention tool. Tax incentives to encourage such work in protected areas and other subsidies provided by the national housing agency in France are good exemplars of financial support for the rehabilitation of buildings in a sensitive manner on the basis that the owner will let the improved property for a minimum period (the so-called renovation lease).

Other intervention tools may operate by defining property rights in ways that make it easier for the private sector to engage in socially desirable transactions involving heritage assets. Easements, restrictive covenants or other enforceable agreements to safeguard buildings, backed by an administration or endowment fund, have been reviewed according to practice in North America; linked to these are enabling procedures transferring development rights or linking development with conservation projects, which can provide an opportunity for funding, but also require adequate safeguards.

Concerning financial measures, many governments have budgetary limitations that make it difficult to justify subsidy programmes and fiscal incentives. For this reason a number of alternative revenue-raising methods have been highlighted in Chapter 2, for example, the use of public lotteries for cultural purposes as in Germany and the United Kingdom. However, studies (though limited in number) have shown that financially supporting the heritage brings benefits, not just to the heritage but indirectly by improving people's quality of life, by sustainable actions such as recycling heritage buildings for new uses, by generating new businesses and new homes as well training and employment, and through tourism. Moreover, in the Netherlands (see Chapter 2) an agreement to expand heritage funding arose out of studies that showed that such action would result in the payment of 8% more tax revenue. Studies in Canada, USA, UK and Germany have come to the same conclusion.

Despite limited financial provisions, most countries in western Europe and North America give grant aid and tax incentives in some form or another as evidenced in chapters 3 and 5. Moreover, different mechanisms can often be combined to great effect, such as in the Netherlands where grant aid, tax incentives and low-interest loans may be combined and advantage may be taken of the Monument Watch system of subsidised surveys as a form of pro-active action to encourage good maintenance/conservation practice rather than wait and undertake more costly restoration projects. This positive mechanism is often linked to financial help. Furthermore, prioritising limited finance is often important, such as directing limited resources at heritage assets found to be most at risk.

The wider economic and social benefits of supporting the heritage through debt programmes (raising money through bond financing) has been proved in the USA. Pooling the credit standing of local governments to borrow money on more favourable terms can be effective. In other respects low-interest loan facilities, such as through revolving fund mechanisms, are also effective, but may require credit safeguards, as is the case with building preservation trusts in the United Kingdom, where a first charge over a building to be repaired and rehabilitated is required. In other respects, the removal of discriminatory practices by lending institutions, as shown by examples in the USA, may be a step forward in favour of loan support to the built heritage, particularly in deprived areas.

This publication has also sought to identify specific measures to promote sponsorship. The National Trust in the United Kingdom provides a good example of the use of tax benefits in relation to the charitable purpose of supporting the heritage as a matter of public interest. Likewise, apart from individual donations, companies can have a role to play in supporting the heritage, as evidenced by examples from Germany and France. In Denmark, foundations can provide funds on top of state aid to ensure that conservation projects are affordable.

This publication has sought to highlight different practices in Europe and North America. The exchange of information in this field may assist in developing new techniques for financially supporting the architectural heritage.

References

Aga Khan Trust for Culture (2004) *The Cultural Agency of the Aga Khan Development Network* (Brochure).

Aga Khan Trust for Culture (2004) *Conservation and Revitalisation of Historic Mostar*, Historic Cities Support Programme (Brochure).

Aga Khan Trust for Culture (2007) *The Cultural Agency of the Aga Khan Development Network* (Brochure).

Allison, G., Ball, S., Cheshire, P., Evans, A. and Stabler, M. (1996) *The Value of Conservation? A Literature Review of the Economic and Social Value of the Cultural Built Heritage*. The Department of National Heritage, English Heritage, The Royal Institution of Chartered Surveyors.

ANAH (1998) *Les actions de l'ANAH en faveur du logement des personnes défavourisées: Des logement locatifs très sociaux dans le parc privé*, Association Nationale Pour L'Amélioration De L'Habitat, Paris.

Andersen, S. (2002) *Evaluation of the Danish Urban Renewal Legislation*. Danish Building and Urban Research Institute (By of Byg), Denmark (Research paper No. 18).

Antolović, J. (2001) *Financing the protection and preservation of the architectural heritage: the Croatian experience*, Proceedings of an international seminar organised by UNESCO under the theme of "Management of Private Property in the Historic City Centres of European Countries in Transition", Bucharest, Romania, 25-29 April 2001.

Antolović, J. (2005) *Monument Annuity from Theory to Croatian Practice*, Ministry of Culture, Zagreb, Croatia.

Antolović, J. (2007) "Monument Annuity as an Economic Tool, and Its Application to Croatia", *Cultural Trends*, Vol. 16, No. 4, December 2007, pp. 301-21.

Architectural Heritage Fund (2002) *Funds for Historic Buildings in England and Wales: A Directory of Sources*. London (see also www.ffhb.org.uk).

Architectural Heritage Fund (2007) *Annual Review, 2006–07*, London.

Aristotelous-Cleridou, A. (2003) Cyprus State of Art Report: Cultural Heritage Issues in relation to Urban Planning Workshop (available at www.arcchip.cz/w03/w03_cleridou.pdf).

Auer, M. (1996) *Preservation Tax Incentives for Historic Buildings.* US Department of the Interior, National Park Service, Cultural Resources, Heritage Preservation Services.

Baltimore City Commission for Historical and Architectural Preservation (1996) *Baltimore City's Tax Credit for Historic Restorations and Rehabilitations.*

Barber, S. (1997) "The Story on the Ground", in *Lightening The Burden: Taxation, Regulation and Heritage Property.* Proceedings of the Heritage Canada Foundation Annual Conference Ottawa, Ontario, 16-18 October 1997.

Barber, T. (2000) "Funding Heritage-Led Regeneration", *Context*, No. 68 (December), pp. 16-18.

Beaumont, C. (1996) *Smart States Better Communities.* National Trust for Historic Preservation.

Beauvais, R. (1999) "Revenus fonciers: Régime des monuments historiques privés", *Vielles Maisons Françaises*, No. 176, pp. 93-6.

Beauvais, R. (2000) "Revenus fonciers: Régime des monuments historiques privés", *Vielles Maisons Françaises*, No. 181, pp. 89-92.

Beernaert, B. and Desimpelaere, W. (2001) "Bruges, Belgium", in Pickard, R. D. (ed.) (2001) *Management of Historic Centres.* Spon Press, London and New York.

Benhamou, F. (1996) "Is Increased Public Spending for the Preservation of Historic Monuments Inevitable? The French Case", *Journal of Cultural Economics*, Vol. 20, pp. 115-31.

Benhamou, F. (1997) "Conserving Historic Monuments in France: A Critique of Official Policies", in Hutter, M. and Rizzo, I. (eds) (1997) *Economic Perspectives on Cultural Heritage*, Macmillan, London, pp. 196-210.

Bergin, F. (1997) "What are the Rules and Who Bears the Burden?" in *Lightening The Burden: Taxation, Regulation and Heritage Property*. Proceedings of the Heritage Canada Foundation Annual Conference, Ottawa, Ontario, 16-18 October 1997.

Blake, J.L. and Lowe, S. (1992) *Using the Community Reinvestment Act in Low Income Historic Neighbourhoods*. National Trust for Historic Preservation, Information Series Number 56.

Borgal, C. (1997) "The Building Code: What is needed to give conservation a break?" in *Lightening The Burden: Taxation, Regulation and Heritage Property*. Proceedings of the Heritage Canada Foundation Annual Conference Ottawa, Ontario, 16-18 October 1997.

Boyle, J.F., Ginsberg, S., Oldham, S.G. and Rypkema, D.D. (1994) *A Guide to Tax Advantage Rehabilitation*. Preservation Information, National Trust for Historic Preservation.

Bridgman, W. and Bridgman, R. (1999) "Heritage Conservation Tax Incentives in Winnipeg", *Heritage – The Magazine of the Heritage Canada Foundation* (Spring), pp. 18-20.

Brown, W. (1997) "What are the Rules and Who Bears the Burden?" in *Lightening The Burden: Taxation, Regulation and Heritage Property*. Proceedings of the Heritage Canada Foundation Annual Conference, Ottawa, Ontario, 16-18 October 1997.

Brown, W. (1999) "Nova Scotia's Sales Tax Rebate Program for Heritage Property Owners", *Heritage – The Magazine of the Heritage Canada Foundation* (Fall), pp. 29-30.

Bruggemann, S. and Schwarzkopf, C. (2001) "Germany", in Pickard, R. (ed.) *Policy and Law in Heritage Conservation*. Spon Press, London and New York.

Burman, P., Pickard, R. Taylor, S. (1995) (eds) *The Economics of Architectural Conservation*, Institute of Advanced Architectural Studies, The University of York.

Byrtus, N. and McClelland, M. (2000) *U.S. Preservation Tax Incentives: An Overview with Case Studies*. ERA Architects Inc.

Calvo, M.S.M. (2001) "Spain", in Pickard, R. (ed.) (2001) *Policy and Law in Heritage Conservation*. Spon Press, London and New York, pp. 265-88.

Chouinard, C. (1997) "The Income Tax Act, What are the Problems? What are the Alternatives?" in *Lightening The Burden: Taxation, Regulation and Heritage Property*. Proceedings of the Heritage Canada Foundation Annual Conference, Ottawa, Ontario, 16-18 October 1997.

City of Edmonton (1988) "Policy to Encourage the Designation and Rehabilitation of Municipal Historic Resource in Edmonton", City Policy number C-450, City Procedure, City of Edmonton, Canada.

City of Edmonton (1997) "The Historic Resource Management Programme" in *Information Pack i). Working with reality at the local level – Taxation, Regulation and Heritage Property; ii). Policy to encourage the Designation and Rehabilitation of municipal historic resources in Edmonton – heritage tax policy; iii). Council report and municipal historic resource Designation by-law; iv). Compensation agreement; v). Maintenance agreement; vi). Does provincial legislation permit municipal tax rebates for heritage properties?.*

Cliver, B.E. (1997) "National Register and Conservation Standards: Meeting the Need" in *Lightening The Burden: Taxation, Regulation and Heritage Property*. Proceedings of the Heritage Canada Foundation Annual Conference, Ottawa, Ontario, 16-18 October 1997.

The Conservation Practice (1992) *The Grainger Town Study: Stage 1 Report,* English Heritage, Newcastle City Council and the Department of Environment Inner City Partnership.

Cornu, M., Férault, M.-A. and Fromageau, J. (eds) (2003): *Patrimoine architectural, urbain et paysager: enjeux juridiques et dynamiques territoriales*, Actes du colloque organisé par la direction de l'architecture et du patrimoine du ministère de la culture et de la communication, en partenariat avec groupe de recherche sur le droit du patrimoine culturel et naturel et l'association patrimoine rhônalpin, Editions l'Harmattan, Paris.

Costonis, J. (1974) *Space Adrift: Landmark Preservation and the Marketplace*, National Trust for Historic Preservation, University of Illinois Press.

Costonis, J. (1997) "The Redefinition of Property Rights as a Tool for Historic Preservation" in Schuster, M., de Monchaux, J. and Riley, C.A. (eds), *Preserving the Built Heritage: Tools for Implementation*, Salzburg Seminar, University Press of New England, Hanover, NH.

Council of Europe (1966) *Resolution 66 (20) on the reviving of monuments*, adopted by the Ministers' Deputies on 29 March 1966.

Council of Europe (1975) *Amsterdam Declaration*, proclaimed at the Congress on the European Architectural Heritage (Amsterdam, 21-25 October 1975).

Council of Europe (1976) *Resolution 76 (28) concerning the adaptation of laws and regulations to the requirements of integrated conservation of the architectural heritage*, adopted by the Committee of Ministers on 14 April 1976.

Council of Europe (1985) *Convention for the Protection of the Architectural Heritage in Europe* (Granada, 3 October 1985), ETS, No. 121 (Granada Convention).

Council of Europe (1987) *Funding the Architectural Heritage. Report of the York Colloquy, Architectural Heritage Reports and Studies No. 8.* Council of Europe Publishing, Strasbourg.

Council of Europe (1988) *New Ways of Funding the Restoration of the Architectural Heritage. Report of the Messina Colloquy, Architectural Heritage Reports and Studies No. 13.* Council of Europe Publishing, Strasbourg.

Council of Europe (1991) *Funding the Architectural Heritage.* Council of Europe in collaboration with the Association of Italian Savings Banks and National Centre of French Savings Banks. Council of Europe Publications, Strasbourg.

Council of Europe (1991) *Recommendation No. R (91) 6 on measures likely to promote the funding of the conservation of the architectural heritage*, adopted by the Committee of Ministers on 11 April 1991.

Council of Europe (2000) *Guidance on the development of legislation and administrative systems in the field of cultural heritage.* Technical Co-operation and Consultancy Programme, Council of Europe Publications, Strasbourg.

Council of Europe (2002) *European Cultural Heritage (Volume I) Intergovernmental Co-operation: collected texts*, Council of Europe Publications, Strasbourg.

Council of Europe (2002) *Urban Rehabilitation Policy in Tbilisi (Georgia)*, Council of Europe Publications, Strasbourg.

Council of Europe (2003) *Resolution 1355 (2003) Tax incentives for cultural heritage conservation*, adopted by the Standing Committee, acting on behalf of the Parliamentary Assembly, on 25 November 2003.

Council of Europe (2003) *Recommendation 1634 (2003) Tax incentives for cultural heritage conservation*, adopted by the Standing Committee, acting on behalf of the Parliamentary Assembly, on 25 November 2003.

Council of Europe (2005) *Recommendation 1730 (2005) The private management of cultural property*, adopted by the Standing Committee, acting on behalf of the Parliamentary Assembly, on 25 November 2005.

Council of Europe Development Bank (2006) *Policy for Loan and Project Financing*.

Council of Europe Development Bank (2007) *Annual Report*.

Coussy, B. (2001) "Rochefort, France" in Pickard, R. (ed.) (2001) *Management of Historic Centres*. Spon Press, London and New York.

Cyprus *see* Republic of Cyprus

Delvac, W.F., Escherich, S. and Hartman, B. (1997) *Affordable Housing through Historic Preservation – A Case Study Guide to Combining the Tax Credits*. Government Publication, US Department of the Interior, National Parks Service, Cultural Resources, Heritage Preservation Services, National Trust for Historic Preservation.

Denhez, M.C. (1981) "What Price Heritage?" *Plan Canada*, Vol. 21, No. 1, pp. 5-14.

Denhez, M.C. (1997) *The Heritage Strategy Planning Handbook*. Dundrum Press, Toronto and Oxford.

Denhez, M.C. (1999) *Law, Finance and Organisation*. ICOMOS Canada Committee.

Denhez, M.C. (2000) "Stewardship Through Covenanting – The Canadian Tax Context" in *Proceedings of the University of Calgary Conference*. September, 2000.

Denhez, M. and Dennis, S.N. (1997) "Legal and Financial Aspects of Architectural Conservation" in *Proceedings of the Smolenice Castle Conference Papers 1997*. Dundrum Press, Toronto and Oxford.

Department of Environment and Department of National Heritage (1994) *Planning Policy Guidance 15: Planning and the Historic Environment*, HMSO, London.

Drivas Jonas (2006) *Heritage Works: The use of historic buildings in regeneration: A toolkit of good practice*, Royal Institution of Chartered Surveyors, British Property Federation, English Heritage and Drivas Jonas, London.

Drouin, G. (1997) "The Story on the Ground" in *Lightening The Burden: Taxation, Regulation and Heritage Property*. Proceedings of the Heritage Canada Foundation Annual Conference, Ottawa, Ontario, 16-18 October 1997.

Duerksen, C.J. (ed.) (1983) *A Handbook on Historic Preservation Law*. The Conservation Foundation, The National Center for Preservation Law, USA.

Durnford, J.W. (1997) "The deductibility of building repair and renovation costs". *Canadian Tax Journal*, Vol. 45, No. 3.

EAHTR (2007) *INHERIT – Investing in Heritage: A Guide to Successful Urban Regeneration*, European Association of Historic Towns and Regions, Norwich.

EDAW (1996) *Grainger Town Regeneration Strategy*, Newcastle City Council and English Partnerships, UK.

Eggenkamp, W. (2002) *Stadsherstel Amsterdam N.V., Annual Report*, Amsterdam.

Eggenkamp, W.M.N. and Luigies, B.M. (1997) *The Amsterdam Urban Restoration Company 'Stasherstel'*, Stadsherstel, Amsterdam.

English Heritage (1998) *Conservation-led Regeneration: The Work of English Heritage*. London.

English Heritage (1998) *Buildings at Risk*. London.

English Heritage (1999) *Enabling Development and the Conservation of Heritage Assets*. London.

English Heritage (1999) *Guidance Notes for Applicants – English Heritage Grants for the Repair and Conservation of Historic Buildings, Monuments and Gardens, 1999-2002*. London.

English Heritage (2000) *Power of Place*. London.

English Heritage (2001) *Enabling Development: and the Conservation of Heritage Assets: Policy Statement and Practical Guide to Assessment*. London.

English Heritage (2004) *Grants for Historic Buildings, Monuments and Designed Landscapes*, London.

English Heritage (2004) *Funding for Local Authorities: Partnership Schemes in Conservation Areas*, London.

English Heritage (2005) *Regeneration and the Historic Environment*, London.

English Heritage (2005) *Valuation of the Historic Environment*, London.

English Heritage (2005) *Low Demand Housing and the Historic Environment*, London (position statement).

English Heritage (2006) *Heritage Counts: The State of England's Historic Environment 2006 (Executive Summary)*, London.

English Heritage, Town Centres Ltd. and London School of Economics (1999) *The Heritage Dividend*, English Heritage, London.

English Heritage and Urban Practitioners (2002) *Heritage Dividend 2002*, English Heritage, London.

Enotiades, P. (2001) *Documentation, Interpretation and Presentation of the Architectural Heritage of Cyprus* (available at http://www.eukn.org/eukn/themes/Urban_Policy/Urban_environment/Cultural_heritage/architectural-heritage-of-cyprus_1001.html).

Escherich, S.M., Farneth, S.J. and Judd, B.D. (1997) *Affordable Housing through Historic Preservation: Tax Credits and the Secretary of the Interior's Standards for Historic Rehabilitation*, US Department of the Interior, National Park Service, Washington DC.

Estévez, X. (2001) "Santiago de Compostela, Spain" in Pickard, R.D. (ed.) *Management of Historic Centres*. Spon Press, London and New York.

EUCLID (2007) *Culture Delivers*, EUCLID Publications, Manchester.

European Commission (2003) *Partnership with the Cities: The Urban Community Initiative*, European Union Regional Policy Brochure.

European Commission (2006) *The Economy of Culture in Europe*.

European Commission (2007) *Instrument for Pre-accession Assistance (IPA) Bosnia and Herzegovina, Multi-Annual Indicative Planning Document 2007-2009* (Commission Decision C(2007) 2255 of 01/06/2007).

European Commission (2007) *Instrument for Pre-accession Assistance (IPA) Albania, Multi-Annual Indicative Planning Document 2007-2009* (Commission Decision C(2007)2245 of 31/05/2007).

European Union (2006) Regulation (EC) No. 1080/2006 of the European Parliament and of the Council of 5 July 2006 on the European Regional Development Fund and repealing Regulation (EC) No. 1783/1999, *Official Journal of the European Union*, L 210/1, 31.7.2006.

Férault, M.-A. (2001) *Les Zones de protection du patrimoine architectural, urbain et paysager: ZZPAUP*, Ministère de la Culture et de la Communication/Ministère de l'Aménagement, France.

Fitch, J.M. (1990) *Historic Preservation: Curatorial Management of the Built World*. University Press of Virginia, Charlottesville and London.

Flitner, H. (1997) "Organizational forms for private sponsorship in Germany" in ICOMOS (1997) *Legal Structures of Private Sponsorship*, Proceedings of an international seminar organised by the German National Committee of ICOMOS in collaboration with the Department of Intellectual and Cultural Property Law of the Faculty of Law and Administration of the University of Katowice, Poland, 17-19 April 1997, Weimar, Germany, at pp. 43-7.

Fram, M. (1997) "National Register and Conservation Standards: Meeting the Need" in *Lightening The Burden: Taxation, Regulation and Heritage Property*. Proceedings of the Heritage Canada Foundation Annual Conference, Ottawa, Ontario, 16-18 October 1997.

Franklin, D. (1997) "Tax Treatment of Heritage Property in Canada" in *Lightening The Burden: Taxation, Regulation and Heritage Property*. Proceedings of the Heritage Canada Foundation Annual Conference, Ottawa, Ontario, 16-18 October 1997.

Fraser, D. (1997) "Working with Reality at the Local Level: Municipal Taxation and Regulation", workshop presentation at the Heritage Canada Foundation 1997 Annual Conference, Ottawa, Canada, 16-18 October 1997.

Frey, B.S. (1997) "The Evaluation of Cultural Heritage: Some Critical Issues" in Hutter, M., and Rizzo, I. (eds) (1997), *Economic Perspectives on Cultural Heritage*. MacMillan, London.

Fritz, W. (1997) "Foundations" in *Proceedings on Legal Structures of Private Sponsorship and Participation in the Protection and Maintenance of Monuments*. ICOMOS. Weimar, Germany, 17-19 April 1997, pp. 16-21.

Fritz, W. (1997) "Regulatory Hurdles in Conserving Heritage Property in Canada" in *Lightening The Burden: Taxation, Regulation and Heritage Property*. Proceedings of the Heritage Canada Foundation Annual Conference, Ottawa, Ontario, 16-18 October 1997.

Gianighian, G. (2001) "Italy" in Pickard, R. (ed.) *Policy and Law in Heritage Conservation*. Spon Press, London and New York.

Goblet, M. (1999) *Report on Financing the Architectural Heritage in Belgium*. Cultural Heritage Committee, Council of Europe. AT (99) 006/TE9900150, Strasbourg. Council of Europe (unpublished).

Goblet, M., Cortembos, T., Verhaegen, P., Draye, A.M., Van Reybroeck, J.P. and Joris, F. (2001) "Belgium" in Pickard R. (ed.) (2001) *Policy and Law in Heritage Conservation*. Spon Press, London and New York.

Grainger Town Partnership (1998) *SRB Challenge Fund: Round 3 – Year 2 Delivery Plan 1998/1999*, UK.

Grainger Town Partnership (1999) *SRB Challenge Fund: Round 3 – Year 3 Delivery Plan 1999/2000*, UK.

Grainger Town Partnership (2000) *SRB Challenge Fund: Round 3 – Year 4 Delivery Plan 2000/2001*, UK.

Grainger Town Partnership (2003) *Grainger Town, 1997-2003: Final Report*, UK.

Great Britain, Department for Culture, Media and Sport (2006) *Government Response to the Culture, Media and Sport Committee Report on Protecting and Preserving our Heritage*, London: The Stationery Office (Cm. 6947) at pp. 16-17.

Great Britain, Parliament, House of Commons (2006) *Protecting and Preserving our Heritage, Culture Media and Sport Committee, Third Report of Session 2005–6*, London: The Stationery Office (HC 912-1) at pp. 59-63.

Grimmer, A. and Kay, D. (1992) *The Secretary of the Interior's Standards for Rehabilitation and Illustrated Guidelines for Rehabilitating Historic Buildings*, US Department of the Interior, National Park Service, Cultural Resources, Preservation Assistance Division.

Hahn, M. (1989) *Revenue Ruling – Recapture under Section 47 of the Code*. Internal Revenue Service, Corporation Tax Division, West Group, USA.

Haubroe, H., Hoesch, A., Møller, I. and Høyer, K. R. (1996): *BYFOs Bog om Bygningsfredning: Håndbog for ejere af fredede bygninger*, BYFO, Denmark.

Heritage Canada Foundation (1998) *Heritage of Place*. Policy Brief, Canada.

Heritage Canada Foundation (1999) *Response to the Federal Cultural Policy Report*.

Heritage Canada Foundation (2007) *Federal Incentives needed to encourage private sector investment in Historic Places* (http://www.heritagecanadaorg/pdf/FederalFinancialIncentives/pdf).

Heritage Lottery Fund (1998) *Application Pack*, UK.

Heritage Lottery Fund (1999) *Strategic Plan 1999-2002*, UK.

Heritage Lottery Fund (2001) *Corporate Plan 2001*, UK.

Heritage Lottery Fund (2001) *Townscape Heritage Initiative*, UK.

Heritage Lottery Fund (2004) *New Life: Heritage and Regeneration*, UK.

Heritage Lottery Fund (2007) *Our Heritage, Our Future: Towards the Heritage Lottery Fund's Third Strategic Plan, 2008-2013*, UK.

Heritage Preservation Services (1999) *Federal Tax Incentives for Rehabilitating Historic Buildings – Annual Report for Fiscal Year 1998*. Technical Preservation Services, Department of the Interior, National Park Service and the Center for Cultural Resources Stewardship and Partnerships, USA.

Heritage Society of British Columbia and the Victoria Civic Heritage Trust (2000) *The Legacy of Downtown Heritage Revitalisation.*

Hill, J. (1997) "The Company Structure" in *Proceedings on Legal Structures of Private Sponsorship and Participation in the Protection and Maintenance of Monuments*. ICOMOS. Weimar, Germany, 17-19 April 1997, pp. 10-13.

Baroness Hooper (2003) *Tax incentives for cultural heritage conservation*, Report to the Committee on Culture, Science and Education, Doc.9913 rev., for debate in the Standing Committee of the Parliamentary Assembly, Council of Europe, 13 November 2003.

Howard, C.C. (2002) "Tax Expenditures" in Salamon, L.M. (ed.), *The Tools of Government: A Guide to New Governance*. Oxford University Press.

Howlett, M. (1991) "Policy Instruments, Policy Styles and Policy Implementation: National Approaches to Theories of Instrumental Choice". *Policy Studies Journal*, Vol. 19, No. 2, pp. 1-21.

Hutchings, J. (2000) "Saskatoon Heritage Conservation Programme". *Heritage – The Magazine of the Heritage Canada Foundation* (Winter).

ICOMOS (1993) *Economics of Conservation*: Proceedings of the International Scientific Symposium, 10th General Assembly, Sri Lanka.

ICOMOS (1997) *Legal Structures of Private Sponsorship and Participation in the Protection and Maintenance of Monuments*: Proceedings of the International Seminar, Weimar, Germany, 17-19 April 1997.

Indecon International Consultants (2004) *Examination of the Issue of Trust-type Organisations to Manage Heritage Properties in Ireland*, Report prepared for the Department of the Environment, Heritage and Local Government, November 2004, at pp. 72-83. (http://www.environ.ie/DOEI/doeipub.nsf/wvInfoView/17407B65C95D10D280256F0F003DB979?OpenDocument&Lang=en#i2)

Internal Revenue Service (1987) *Rehabilitation Tax Credit, Market Segment Specialisation Programme (MSSP)*, Department of the Treasury, United States.

Investment Property Databank, English Heritage and Royal Institution of Chartered Surveyors (1993) *The Investment Performance of Listed Buildings*, Investment Property Databank, UK (annual updates).

Jamieson, W. (1997) "Provincial Planning Legislation: Cutting the Red Tape for Conservation" in *Lightening The Burden: Taxation, Regulation and Heritage Property*. Proceedings of the Heritage Canada Foundation Annual Conference, Ottawa, Ontario, 16-18 October 1997.

Jeremy Eckstein Associates (1999) *VAT and the Built Heritage: The impact of VAT on repairs and alterations to listed property*, A survey and report commissioned by the Tax Group of the Joint Committee of National Amenity Societies, October 1999. (www.vatbuiltheritage.org.uk)

Johnstone, L. (2004): *Tax credits and other incentives for Heritage Protection in the USA*, Institute of Historic Building Conservation Yearbook 2004, Cathedral Communications Limited, Tisbury, England, at pp. 31-4.

Jokine, E. (1997) "The Building Code: What is needed to give conservation a break?" in *Lightening The Burden: Taxation, Regulation and Heritage Property*, Heritage Canada Foundation Annual Conference, Ottawa, Ontario, 16-18 October 1997.

Kearns, P. (1997) "Monuments in the Law of Trusts" in *Proceedings on Legal Structures of Private Sponsorship and Participation in the Protection and Maintenance of Monuments*. ICOMOS. Weimar, Germany, 17-19 April 1997, at pp. 21-4.

Keefer, M. (1999) "Ontario's Heritage at Risk: The Case of the Eden Mills Bowstring Bridge", *Heritage – The Magazine of the Heritage Canada Foundation* (Spring), pp. 13-15.

Kettle, D.F. (1987) *The Regulation of American Federalism*. Johns Hopkins University Press, Baltimore.

King, T.F (1990) *What is Section 106 Review?* Local Preservation, Interagency Resources Division, Government Publications, Washington DC.

Kirschbaum, J. and Klein, A. (eds) (2000): *Denkmalpflege und Beschäftigung* ("Heritage Conservation and Employment"), Proceedings of an international conference in the framework of the German EU Presidency, 15-16 April 1999 in Berlin, Schriftenreihe des Deutschen Nationalkomitees für Denkmalschutz.

Klamer, A. and Zuidhof, P.W. (1999) "The Value of Cultural Heritage: Merging Economics and Cultural Appraisals" in *Economics and Heritage Conservation*. Getty Conservation Institute.

Knight, J. (1997) "What are the Rules and Who Bears the Burden?" in *Lightening The Burden: Taxation, Regulation and Heritage Property*. Proceedings of the Heritage Canada Foundation Annual Conference, Ottawa, Ontario, 16-18 October 1997.

Kobalt, C. (1997) "Optimising the Use of Cultural Heritage" in Hutter, M. and Rizzo, I. (eds), *Economic Perspectives on Cultural Heritage*. MacMillan, London.

Legg Mason Realty Group and Government Finance Group (1996) *The Economic and Fiscal Impacts of Rehabilitation Projects Assisted with Maryland Historical Trust, Historic Preservation Grants and Loans*. Maryland Historical Trust.

Lichfield, N. (1993) "Social and Economic Aspects of Monument Preservation" in *Proceedings of the International Association for Bridge and Structural Engineering*, Symposium Italy, Rome, 1993, at pp. 29-42.

Limassol (Lemesos) Municipality (1998) *Historic Preservation: Sea Front Old and New Harbour* (available at: http://www.limassolmunicipal.com.cy/sea/historic.html).

Lipman, Frizzell and Mitchell (1998) *Local Historic Districts. Economic and Fiscal Impacts – Six Case Studies*. Maryland Association of Historic District Commissioners, USA.

Listokin, D. and Lahr, M.L. (1997) *Economic Impacts of Historic Preservation*. Center for Urban Policy Research Report No. 16. Rutgers State University, USA.

Listokin, D. and Lahr, M. (2001) "How Preservation Pays in the United States" in *Preservation Pays: the Economics of Heritage Conservation. Proceedings of the Heritage Canada Foundation Conference, Toronto (October 11-13) 2001*.

Loew, S. (1998) *Modern Architecture in Historic Cities: Policy, planning and building in contemporary France*, Routledge, London and New York.

Longuet, I. and Vincent, J.M. (2001) "France" in Pickard, R. (ed.) *Policy and Law in Heritage Conservation*. Spon Press, London and New York.

Look, D.W., Wong, T. and Augustus, S.R. (1997) *The Seismic Retrofit of Historic Buildings: Keeping Preservation in the Forefront*. US Department of the Interior, National Park Service, Cultural Resources, Heritage Preservation Service.

Lovie, D. (2001) "Grainger Town, Newcastle upon Tyne, United Kingdom" in Pickard, R. (ed.) *Management of Historic Centres*. Spon Press, London and New York.

Lowenthal, D. (2000) "Stewarding the Past in a Perplexing Present" in *Values and Heritage Conservation*. Research Report, Getty Conservation Institute.

Lunn, U. and Lund, C. (2001) "Denmark" in Pickard, R. (ed.), *Policy and Law in Heritage Conservation*. Spon Press, London and New York.

MacRory, R. and Kirwan, S. (2001) "Ireland" in Pickard, R. (ed.) *Policy and Law in Heritage Conservation*. Spon Press, London and New York, at pp. 158-83.

Marcon, C. (1999) "Adaptive Reuse of Heritage Buildings. Social Changes and Heritage Strategies" in *Proceedings of The Heritage Canada Foundation Annual Conference*, St. John's, Newfoundland, 21-23 October 1999.

Marcus, N. (1984) *Air Rights in New York City: TDR Zoning Lot Merger and the Well Considered Plan*. Brooklyn, USA.

Maryland Heritage Area Authority (1997) *Annual Report*, Maryland, USA.

Maryland Historical Trust (1996) *Maryland Heritage Preservation and Tourism Areas Programme*. Maryland Department of Housing and Community Development, USA.

Maryland Historical Trust (1996) *Summary of Direct and Indirect Financial Assistance Programmes*. Office of Preservation Services, USA.

Mason, R. (1999) "Economics and Heritage Conservation: Concepts, Values and Agendas for Research" in *Economics and Heritage Conservation*, Getty Conservation Institute.

Mason, R. (2002) "Assessing Values in Conservation Planning: Methodological Issues and Choices" in *Assessing the Value of Cultural Heritage*, Research Report, Getty Conservation Institute.

McCleary, R.L. (2005) *Financial Incentives for Historic Preservation: An International View*, University of Pennsylvania (http://repository.upenn.edu/hp theses/35).

McDonald, B. (1998) "Opportunity Lost – Steel Plant Falls to Wreckers – Vancouver's Canron Building", *Heritage – The Magazine of the Heritage Canada Foundation* (Spring 1998).

Mendelsohn, J. (1998) *Twenty-five years of Preserving New York, 1973 to 1998*. New York Landmarks Conservatory.

Miller, M.G. (2000) "Edmonton's New Market Value Assessments", *Heritage – The Magazine of the Heritage Canada Foundation* (Winter 2000), pp. 18-22.

Minister of the Environment, Minister of Supply and Services Canada (1982) *Policy on Federal Heritage Buildings*. Government Publications, Canada.

Mitchell, R. (1996) "The Appraisal of National Cultural Policies, a Council of Europe Programme – The Dilemma of Cross-National Comparisons" [1st part], *Circular: Research and Documentation on Cultural Policies*, CIRCLE Newsletter, No. 3.

Moriarity, H.L. and Lutzker, S.J. (1993) *National Trust for Historic Preservation*. Information Series No. 78.

Morton, H. (1993) "Update on US Rehabilitation Tax Credits and the Transfer of Development Rights" in ICOMOS (1993) *Economics of Conservation*: Proceedings of the International Scientific Symposium, 10th General Assembly, Sri Lanka.

MSV (1992) *Denkmäler erhalten – der Staat hilft Steuertips für Dekmaleigentümer*, 4/92, Ministerium für Stadtentwicklung und Verkehr des Landes Nordrhein-westfalen, Dusseldorf.

Murray, G. (1998) *Historic Buildings, Downtown Decline, Taxes and Choices*. Paper addressed to Winnipeg City Council (16 January 1998).

Mynors, C. (1999) *Listed Buildings, Conservation Areas and Monuments*, 3rd edn, Sweet and Maxwell, London.

National Park Service (1990) *The Secretary of the Interior's Standards for Rehabilitation and Guidelines for Rehabilitating Historic Buildings*, US Department of the Interior, National Park Service, Washington DC.

National Park Service (1994) *Federal Lands to Parks Program and Historic Surplus Property Program – New Uses for Federal Properties*, US Department of the Interior.

National Park Service (1996) *Questions and Answers about Certified Local Government Grants from State Historic Preservation Officers – An Introductory Guide*. Heritage Preservation Services, US Department of the Interior, Cultural Resources.

National Park Service (1997): *Preservation Economic Impact Model 2.0*, National Center for Preservation Technology and Training, Publication No. 1997-05, US Department of the Interior.

National Parks Service (1998) *Federal Tax Incentives for Rehabilitating Historic Buildings, Statistical Report and Analysis for Fiscal Year 1997*, Government Publication – US Department of the Interior, Cultural Resource Stewardship and Partnerships, Heritage Preservation Services Programme, Technical Preservation Services Branch, Washington DC.

National Parks Service (1998) *Millennium Grants – To Save American Treasures*. Government Publication – US Department of the Interior, Cultural Resource Stewardship and Partnerships, Heritage Preservation Services Washington DC.

National Trust for Historic Preservation (1997) *Preservation Advocacy News*, Vol. 9, Department of Law and Public Policy, USA.

National Trust for Historic Preservation (2000) *Preservation Fiscal Year 2000 Appropriations*. Preservation Advocacy, Historic Preservation Fund.

Netzer, D. (1978) *The Subsidized Muse: Public Support for the Arts in the United States*. Cambridge University Press, Cambridge and New York.

New Jersey Historic Trust (1997) *Annual Report 1997.*

New York Landmarks Conservatory (1997) *Annual Report 1997.*

New York Landmarks Conservancy (1998) *Historic Properties Fund*, USA.

Ontario Heritage Policy Review (1990) *Technical Paper No. 2*, Toronto.

Ost, C. and Van, N. (1998) *Report on Economics of Conservation: An Appraisal of Theories, Principles and Methods.* International Economics Committee, ICOMOS.

Pacte de Paris (2000) *OPAH du Bas Belleville, Report D'Activities 1999*, Pacte de Paris, France.

Palmer, N. (1997) "Non-Corporate Voluntary Associations" in *Proceedings on Legal Structures of Private Sponsorship and Participation in the Protection and Maintenance of Monuments.* ICOMOS, Weimar, Germany, 17-19 April 1997, pp. 13-16.

Parker, P.L. (1987) *What are the National Register Criteria?*, Local Preservation, Inter-agency Resources Division, Government Publications, Washington DC.

Parker, P.L. (1987) *What is the National Historic Preservation Act?*, Local Preservation, Inter-agency Resources Division, Government Publications, Washington DC.

Peltier, I. (2006) *Troyes et L'Aube*, Les Éditions de la Maison du Boulanger, France.

Pencek, B. (1994) "Cash in Your Pocket? – Tax Incentives for Historic Property Rehabilitation", *The Phoenix* (newsletter of Preservation Maryland), Vol. 13, No. 1.

Pendlebury, J. (2001) "United Kingdom" in Pickard, R. (ed.), *Policy and Law in Heritage Conservation*, Conservation of the European Built Environment Series, Spon Press, London and New York.

Pennsylvania Historical and Museum Commission (1998) *Keystone Historic Preservation Grant Guidelines*, USA.

Peterman, W. (2001) "Revitalising the Calumet: A Model for Urban Regeneration?" in *Area based Initiatives in Contemporary Urban Policy. Proceedings from the European Urban Research Association and*

Danish Building and Urban Research Conference, 17-19 May 2001, Copenhagen.

Pickard, R. (ed.) (2001) *Policy and Law in Heritage Conservation*, Spon Press, London and New York.

Pickard, R. (ed.) (2001) *Management of Historic Centres*, Spon Press, London and New York.

Pickard, R. (2002) *European Cultural Heritage, Volume 2: A review of policies and practice*, Council of Europe Publishing, Strasbourg.

Pickard, R. (ed.) (2008) *Sustainable Development Strategies in South-East Europe*, European Heritage Series, Council of Europe Publishing, Strasbourg.

Pickard, R. and Pickerill, T. (2002) *Real Estate Tax Credits and Other Financial Incentives for Investing in Historic Property in the United States*, RICS Foundation Research Paper, Vol. 4, No. 17, pp. 1-63 (www.rics-foundation.org).

Pickard, R. and Pickerill, T. (2002) "Conservation Finance 1: Support for Historic Buildings", *Structural Survey*, Vol. 20, No. 2, pp. 73-7.

Pickard, R. and Pickerill, T. (2002) "Conservation Finance 2: Area Based Initiatives and the Role of Foundations, Funds and Non-profit Agencies", *Structural Survey*, Vol. 20, No. 4, pp. 112-16.

Pickard, R. and Pickerill, T. (2007) *A Review of Fiscal Measures to Benefit Heritage Conservation*, RICS Research Paper Series Vol. 7, No. 6 (July 2007), pp. 1-59.

Pickerill, T. (2004) "Funding the conservation of the architectural heritage", unpublished PhD thesis, Northumbria University, United Kingdom.

Pignataro, G. and Rizzo, I. (1997) "Heritage Regulation: Regimes, Cases and Effects" in Hutter, M. and Rizzo, I. (eds) (1997), *Economic Perspectives on Cultural Heritage*, MacMillan, London.

Poel, K.W. (1997) "The German Foundation for the Protection of Monuments" in ICOMOS (1997) *Legal Structures of Private Sponsorship*, Proceedings of an International Seminar organised by the German National Committee of ICOMOS in collaboration with the Department of Intellectual and Cultural Property Law of the Faculty of Law and Administration of the University of Katowice, Poland, 17-19 April 1997, Weimar, Germany, at pp. 47-9.

PRA Inc. (2005) *Formative Evaluation of Historic Places Initiative, Final Report*, Parks Canada Agency, March 2005 (available at http://www. pc.gc.ca/docs/pc/rpts/rve-par/pdf/eval_formative_hpi-e.pdf).

Predieri, A. (1988) "Legal Aspects of Restoration and Financing" in Council of Europe (1988) *New Ways of Funding the Restoration of the Architectural Heritage. Report of the Messina Colloquy, Architectural Heritage Reports and Studies No. 13.* Council of Europe Publishing.

Province of British Columbia (1994) *Heritage Conservation: A Community Guide*. BC Government Publication.

Renner, L. and Dugan, N. (1998) *Partners in Prosperity – The Economic Benefits of Historic Preservation in New Jersey*. New Jersey Historic Trust.

Republic of Cyprus (2005) *Urban Policy: Conservation Policy*, Ministry of the Interior, Department of Town Planning and Housing, Republic of Cyprus (available at http://www.eukn.org/cyprus/urban/urbanpolicy/index.html).

Republic of Cyprus (2007) *Citizen's Charter: Land Surveys: Listed Buildings: Applications* (available at http://www.moi.gov.cy/moi/citizens-charter/CitizensCharter.nsf/All/465C9442334D02F1C2256E54003BC E36?OpenDocument).

Reynolds, J. (1980) "Conservation Easements Workshop" in Duerksen C.J. (1983) (ed.) *A Handbook on Historic Preservation Law*. The Conservation Foundation, The National Center for Preservation Law, USA.

Richel-Bottinga, S. (2001) "The Netherlands" in Pickard, R. (ed.), *Policy and Law in Heritage Conservation*. Spon Press, London and New York.

Robinson, F., Dowdy, H., Downie, M.L., Fisher, P. and Greenhalgh, P. (2001) *Investing in Grainger Town – The Renaissance of Newcastle's Grainger Town*. Grainger Town Partnership.

Roddewig, R. and Inghram, C. (1987) "Transfer Development Rights Programs: TDRs and the Real Estate Marketplace", American Planning Association (PAS), Report No. 401.

Rypkema, D. (1994) *The Economics of Historic Preservation – A Community Leader's Guide*. National Trust for Historic Preservation.

Rypkema, D. (2000) *Profiting from the Past: The Impact of Historic Preservation on the North Carolina Economy*. Preservation North Carolina, in the Dollars and Sense of Historic Preservation series, National Trust for Historic Preservation.

Rypkema, D. (2000) *The Value of Historic Preservation in Maryland*, Preservation Maryland, in the Dollars and Sense of Historic Preservation series, National Trust for Historic Preservation.

Rypkema, D., Spatz, I. and Kavlin, M. (1990) *Rehab Takes A Fall*. Historic Preservation – Special Report, National Trust for Historic Preservation.

Rypkema, D. and Wiehagen, K.M. (2000) *The Economic Benefits of Preserving Philadelphia's Past*. Preservation Alliance for Greater Philadelphia, in the Dollars and Sense of Historic Preservation series, National Trust for Historic Preservation.

Scanlon, K., Edge, A. and Willmott, T. (1994) *The Economics of Listed Buildings*, Discussion Paper 43, Department of Land Economy, University of Cambridge.

Schidnidman, F. (1978) "Transfer of Development Rights", in Hagman, D. and Misczynski, D. (eds) (1978) *Windfalls for Wipeouts*, American Society of Planning Officials, Chicago.

Schuster, J.M.D. (1986) "Tax Incentives as Arts Policy in Western Europe" in P.J. DiMaggio (ed.), *Non-profit Enterprise in the Arts: Studies in Mission and Constraint*, Oxford University Press, Oxford and New York.

Schuster, M.J. (1999) "The Other Side of the Subsidized Muse: Indirect Aid Revisited", *Journal of Cultural Economics*, Kluwer Academic Publishers, Vol. 23, pp. 51-70.

Schuster, M.J. (2002) "Making a List and Checking it Twice: The List as a Tool of Historic Preservation", in *Proceedings of the International Association for Cultural Economics*, Bi-annual Conference, Rotterdam, The Netherlands, 13-15 June 2002.

Schuster, M. (2002) "Sub-National Cultural Policy – Where the Action is? Mapping Cultural Policy in the United States, Cultural Sites, Cultural Theory, Cultural Policy" in *Proceedings at The Second International*

Conference on Cultural Policy Research, Wellington, New Zealand 2002.

Schuster, M., de Monchaux, J. and Riley, C.A. (1997), (eds) *Preserving the Built Heritage: Tools for Implementation, Salzburg Seminar*. University Press of New England, Hanover NH.

Shipley, R. (1999) *The Economic Impact of Heritage Conservation*. Simon Fraser University.

Shipley, R. (2001) "Economics of Heritage Conservation" in *Preservation Pays: The Economics of Heritage Conservation*. Proceedings of the Heritage Canada Foundation Conference, Toronto (11-13 October 2001).

Shipley, R. and Bernstein, S. (1998) *Report on Research Trends in Property Values of Designated Heritage Properties in Ontario Communities*. School of Planning, University of Waterloo, Ministry of Citizenship, Culture and Recreation.

Smith, L. (1997) *Historic Preservation Easements – A Historic Preservation Tool with Federal Tax Benefits*. US Department of the Interior, National Park Service, National Center for Cultural Resource Stewardship and Partnerships, Heritage Preservation Services, Technical Preservation Services, Washington DC.

Stanziola, J. (1998) "Modelling the Heritage World: Economic, Legal and Political Considerations", *International Journal of Heritage Studies (IJHS)*, Vol. 3, No. 4, pp. 168-76.

Steel, A.G. (1997) *What is the New York City Landmarks Preservation Commission?* Landmarks Preservation Commission.

Victoria Civic Heritage Trust and HSBC (2000) *The Legacy of Downtown Heritage Revitalisation to Assess the Effectiveness of Victoria's Tax Incentives for residential conversion programmes approved by Council in 1998*. Victoria City Hall.

Wagner, C.P. (2000) "Heritage Economic Regeneration Schemes", *Conservation Bulletin*, Issue 37 (March 2000), English Heritage, London.

Watson, E. and Nagel, S. (1995) *Establishing an Easement Programme to Protect Historic, Scenic and Natural Resources*. National Trust for Historic Preservation.

Weeks, K.D. and Grimmer, A.E. (1995) *The Secretary of the Interior's Standards for the Treatment of Historic Properties with Guidelines for Preserving, Rehabilitating, Restoring and Reconstructing Historic Buildings*. US Department of the Interior, National Park Service, Cultural Resources, Heritage Preservation Services.

Weir, H. (1997) *How to Rescue a Ruin by Setting up a Local Buildings Preservation Trust*, 2nd edn, Architectural Heritage Fund, London.

West, A. (1999) "Fund-raising for Heritage Buildings – The Saint George Experience", *Heritage – The Magazine of the Heritage Canada Foundation* (Summer 1999).

World Bank (1998) *Culture and Sustainable Development: A Framework for Action*.

World Bank (2001) *Cultural Properties in Policy and Practice: A Review of World Bank Experience*, Report No. 23369 (19 December 2001).

World Bank (2004) *Implementation Completion Report (IDA-30400) on a Credit in the Amount of SDR 3.4 million (US $4.49 million equivalent) to Georgia for a Cultural Heritage Project*, Report No: 29316-GE (15 June 2004).

World Bank (2005) *Implementation Completion Report (IDA-32690 TF-39456 TF-23554 TF-23567 TF-50274 TF29809 TF-50257 TF-50455) on a Credit in the Amount of US $4.0 million equivalent to Bosnia and Herzegovina for a Cultural Heritage Pilot*, Report No: 32713 (22 June 2005).

Ziegler, E.H. (1995) "The Transfer of Development Rights" [Part 1], *Zoning and Planning Law Report*, Clark Boardman Callaghan, New York.

Ziegler, E.H. (1995) "The Transfer of Development Rights" [Part 2], *Zoning and Planning Law Report*, Clark Boardman Callaghan, New York.

Internet sources

www.ahfund.org.uk/ Architectural Heritage Fund, United Kingdom

www.brandenburgische-schloesser-gmbh.de/eng/index_eng.html/ Brandenburgische Schlösser GmbH, Germany

www.byfo.dk/ Bygnings Frednings Foreningen (BYFO): Building Care Programme

www.coebank.org/ Council of Europe Development Bank

www.denkmalschutz.de/ Deutsche Stiftung Denkmalschutz: The German Foundation for Monument Protection

www.europanostra.org/ Europa Nostra

www.european-heritage.net/sdx/herein/ European Heritage Network: National Heritage Policies

http://ec.europa.eu/culture/portal/activities/heritage/cultural_heritage_en.htm/ European Cultural Portal

www.ffhb.org.uk/ Funds for Historic Buildings in England and Wales – A Directory of Sources: Architectural Heritage Fund, United Kingdom

www.fondation-patrimoine.com/ Fondation du Patrimoine (Heritage Foundation), France

www.getty.edu/grants/conservation/ The Getty Foundation: Conservation Institute

www.heritagecanada.org/ Heritage Canada Foundation

www.heritagefdn.on.ca/ Ontario Heritage Trust

www.nationaltrust.org.uk/ The National Trust, United Kingdom

www.nylandmarks.org/ The New York Landmarks Conservancy

www.presnc.org/ Preservation North Carolina

www.stadsherstelamsterdam.nl/ Stadsherstel Amsterdam NV

www.wmf.org/ World Monuments Fund

www.worldbank.org/ The World Bank

Index

E

F

Sales agents for publications of the Council of Europe
Agents de vente des publications du Conseil de l'Europe

BELGIUM/BELGIQUE
La Librairie Européenne -
The European Bookshop
Rue de l'Orme, 1
B-1040 BRUXELLES
Tel.: +32 (0)2 231 04 35
Fax: +32 (0)2 735 08 60
E-mail: order@libeurop.be
http://www.libeurop.be

Jean De Lannoy
Avenue du Roi 202 Koningslaan
B-1190 BRUXELLES
Tel.: +32 (0)2 538 43 08
Fax: +32 (0)2 538 08 41
E-mail: jean.de.lannoy@dl-servi.com
http://www.jean-de-lannoy.be

CANADA
Renouf Publishing Co. Ltd.
1-5369 Canotek Road
OTTAWA, Ontario K1J 9J3, Canada
Tel.: +1 613 745 2665
Fax: +1 613 745 7660
Toll-Free Tel.: (866) 767-6766
E-mail: order.dept@renoufbooks.com
http://www.renoufbooks.com

CZECH REPUBLIC/
RÉPUBLIQUE TCHÈQUE
Suweco CZ, s.r.o.
Klecakova 347
CZ-180 21 PRAHA 9
Tel.: +420 2 424 59 204
Fax: +420 2 848 21 646
E-mail: import@suweco.cz
http://www.suweco.cz

DENMARK/DANEMARK
GAD
Vimmelskaftet 32
DK-1161 KØBENHAVN K
Tel.: +45 77 66 60 00
Fax: +45 77 66 60 01
E-mail: gad@gad.dk
http://www.gad.dk

FINLAND/FINLANDE
Akateeminen Kirjakauppa
PO Box 128
Keskuskatu 1
FIN-00100 HELSINKI
Tel.: +358 (0)9 121 4430
Fax: +358 (0)9 121 4242
E-mail: akatilaus@akateeminen.com
http://www.akateeminen.com

FRANCE
La Documentation française
(diffusion/distribution France entière)
124, rue Henri Barbusse
F-93308 AUBERVILLIERS CEDEX
Tél.: +33 (0)1 40 15 70 00
Fax: +33 (0)1 40 15 68 00
E-mail: commande@ladocumentationfrancaise.fr
http://www.ladocumentationfrancaise.fr

Librairie Kléber
1 rue des Francs Bourgeois
F-67000 STRASBOURG
Tel.: +33 (0)3 88 15 78 88
Fax: +33 (0)3 88 15 78 80
E-mail: francois.wolfermann@librairie-kleber.fr
http://www.librairie-kleber.com

GERMANY/ALLEMAGNE
AUSTRIA/AUTRICHE
UNO Verlag GmbH
August-Bebel-Allee 6
D-53175 BONN
Tel.: +49 (0)228 94 90 20
Fax: +49 (0)228 94 90 222
E-mail: bestellung@uno-verlag.de
http://www.uno-verlag.de

GREECE/GRÈCE
Librairie Kauffmann s.a.
Stadiou 28
GR-105 64 ATHINAI
Tel.: +30 210 32 55 321
Fax.: +30 210 32 30 320
E-mail: ord@otenet.gr
http://www.kauffmann.gr

HUNGARY/HONGRIE
Euro Info Service kft.
1137 Bp. Szent István krt. 12.
H-1137 BUDAPEST
Tel.: +36 (06)1 329 2170
Fax: +36 (06)1 349 2053
E-mail: euroinfo@euroinfo.hu
http://www.euroinfo.hu

ITALY/ITALIE
Licosa SpA
Via Duca di Calabria, 1/1
I-50125 FIRENZE
Tel.: +39 0556 483215
Fax: +39 0556 41257
E-mail: licosa@licosa.com
http://www.licosa.com

MEXICO/MEXIQUE
Mundi-Prensa México, S.A. De C.V.
Río Pánuco, 141 Delegacion Cuauhtémoc
06500 MÉXICO, D.F.
Tel.: +52 (01)55 55 33 56 58
Fax: +52 (01)55 55 14 67 99
E-mail: mundiprensa@mundiprensa.com.mx
http://www.mundiprensa.com.mx

NETHERLANDS/PAYS-BAS
De Lindeboom Internationale Publicaties b.v.
M.A. de Ruyterstraat 20 A
NL-7482 BZ HAAKSBERGEN
Tel.: +31 (0)53 5740004
Fax: +31 (0)53 5729296
E-mail: books@delindeboom.com
http://www.delindeboom.com

NORWAY/NORVÈGE
Akademika
Postboks 84 Blindern
N-0314 OSLO
Tel.: +47 2 218 8100
Fax: +47 2 218 8103
E-mail: support@akademika.no
http://www.akademika.no

POLAND/POLOGNE
Ars Polona JSC
25 Obroncow Street
PL-03-933 WARSZAWA
Tel.: +48 (0)22 509 86 00
Fax: +48 (0)22 509 86 10
E-mail: arspolona@arspolona.com.pl
http://www.arspolona.com.pl

PORTUGAL
Livraria Portugal
(Dias & Andrade, Lda.)
Rua do Carmo, 70
P-1200-094 LISBOA
Tel.: +351 21 347 42 82 / 85
Fax: +351 21 347 02 64
E-mail: info@livrariaportugal.pt
http://www.livrariaportugal.pt

RUSSIAN FEDERATION/
FÉDÉRATION DE RUSSIE
Ves Mir
9a, Kolpacnhyi per.
RU-101000 MOSCOW
Tel.: +7 (8)495 623 6839
Fax: +7 (8)495 625 4269
E-mail: orders@vesmirbooks.ru
http://www.vesmirbooks.ru

SPAIN/ESPAGNE
Mundi-Prensa Libros, s.a.
Castelló, 37
E-28001 MADRID
Tel.: +34 914 36 37 00
Fax: +34 915 75 39 98
E-mail: libreria@mundiprensa.es
http://www.mundiprensa.com

SWITZERLAND/SUISSE
Van Diermen Editions – ADECO
Chemin du Lacuez 41
CH-1807 BLONAY
Tel.: +41 (0)21 943 26 73
Fax: +41 (0)21 943 36 05
E-mail: info@adeco.org
http://www.adeco.org

UNITED KINGDOM/ROYAUME-UNI
The Stationery Office Ltd
PO Box 29
GB-NORWICH NR3 1GN
Tel.: +44 (0)870 600 5522
Fax: +44 (0)870 600 5533
E-mail: book.enquiries@tso.co.uk
http://www.tsoshop.co.uk

UNITED STATES and CANADA/
ÉTATS-UNIS et CANADA
Manhattan Publishing Company
468 Albany Post Road
CROTTON-ON-HUDSON, NY 10520, USA
Tel.: +1 914 271 5194
Fax: +1 914 271 5856
E-mail: Info@manhattanpublishing.com
http://www.manhattanpublishing.com

Council of Europe Publishing/Editions du Conseil de l'Europe
F-67075 Strasbourg Cedex
Tel.: +33 (0)3 88 41 25 81 – Fax: +33 (0)3 88 41 39 10 – E-mail: publishing@coe.int – Website: http://book.coe.int